Seven Layers of Successful Relationships

Gino L. Collura, PhD

© 2021 Dr Gino Collura

All rights are reserved as the sole property of the author. The author guarantees all content is original and does not infringe upon the legal rights of any other person or work. No part of this publication may be reproduced, stored in a retrieval system, or transmitted in any form or by any means, electronic, mechanical, photocopying, recording, or otherwise without the prior permission of the author or in accordance with the provisions of the Copyright, Designs, and Patents Act 1988, or under the terms of any license permitting limited copying issued by the Copyright Licensing Agency.

Published by: The Ghost Publishing, USA

Edited by: Eli Gonzalez and Christine James

Book Cover Design: Amanda Wright

Paperback ISBN-13: 978-1-7372350-1-9

Ebook ISBN-13: 978-1-7372350-2-6

Printed in the United States of America

Testimonials

"Far too often we get caught up in what we think versus understanding how we feel. This matters in relationships. Dr. Collura provides a roadmap on how to tap into our deeper selves so we can authentically connect with others in a way that is relatable and very much appropriate for the times we live in. Everyone needs the lessons and insights provided in this book!"

DR. LAUREL GEISE
INTERNATIONAL SPEAKER, AUTHOR
AND CO-FOUNDER OF MMI MINDFUL TRAINING COMPANY

"I wish I had this book when I was commanding troops while fighting the war on terrorism. The nuggets of wisdom and applied understanding that Dr. Collura empowers the reader with highlights so many pitfalls experienced in any and all relationships. It's an outstanding guide on making relationships better by making yourself better."

DR. DAMON FRIEDMAN
LT. COLONEL USAF SPECIAL OPERATIONS (RET)

"I live for connection; it's one of my core values and the foundation of my company. Dr. Gino's teachings have helped me nurture relationships with people from all seven continents. This is more than a book; this is a roadmap to navigate the unexpected and it continues to show up for me in ways I never thought possible."

LAUREN A. KOENIG
CEO & Founder, TWIP

"A refreshing and meaningful guide to all relationships. I recommend it to all of my clients who have experienced relationship challenges!"

DANNY ALVAREZ, ESQ.
DIVORCE AND FAMILY LAW ATTORNEY

"This book and Dr. Collura's approach to relationships has been a cornerstone in my personal and professional life. You truly won't find a better guide to understanding yourself so you can better understand others. A definite must read!"

TRAVIS JENNINGS
FOUNDER AND CEO OF FINANCE CAPE

"I've coached athletes all over the globe and have competed at the highest of levels. Athletes and coaches need this book. Who you have in your camp and who you allow into your life can make or break your performance as a human being. This is a must read!"

RHADI FERGUSON, PHD,
OLY 2004 JUDO OLYMPIAN 4X NATIONAL JUDO CHAMPION PROFESSIONAL MMA COACH, AUTHOR OF "ENHANCE OR DESTROY YOUR ATHLETIC CAREER"

Dedication

I dedicate this book to my mother, father, wife, and daughter. It is their love and unwavering support that has pushed me deeper into my own development so that I may help develop others.

Table of Contents

Preface 13
Foreword 15
Introduction 18
Connected Disconnection 22

Layer One:
YOU **27**

Most Important 28
Pressure Source 31
Who You Belong With 37
Objectivity and Decision Making 39
Hard Truth 43
Reactions 45

Layer Two:
YOUR SOURCE **47**

Belief 48
Decisions Matter, But What Are They Based Upon? ... 58
Battling Moral Decay 64

Layer Three:
ALIGNMENT **69**

Independent Understanding 70
Identity and History 75
Aligning Mental Models 81
Aligning With Others 86
Stop and Think 93

Layer Four:
LISTEN **95**

Everything You Listen to Influences You 96
Your Brain Listening to Others 104
How to Listen to Others 109
Listening to Measure Commitment 113

Layer Five:
COMMUNICATE WITH NEXT STEPS IN MIND **117**

Ikigai 118
Your Next Step Should Always Be an Investment 123
Trust is Communication's Currency 127
Each Step Counts 133

Layer Six:
STAY OPEN TO POSSIBILITIES **137**

Who Do You Want to Be? 138

Knowing When a Relationship Has Been Exhausted..........144
What Life Looks Like When You Limit Possibilities..........151

Layer Seven:
SELF-REGULATION..**155**

Strive for Balance..156
Self-Regulation Starts with Self-Care................................158
Regulating Stress 162
Influence Yourself So You Can Influence Others................169
Organize Your Relationships..172
Full Circle: Meshing Layers..176
The Next Step 180

About the Author..185
Acknowledgments...187
References..188
Recommended Reading...192

Preface

Relationships are hard; that's a fact. The rise of innovative technology has brought about the unintended consequence of isolating people within their own imagination and restricting their perception of the world to what they perceive through social media platforms, apps, and digital conversations. This crack in the fiber of humanity is cloaked within a world of "digital relationships" which are missing the vital components needed to fulfill the human condition and successfully build transparent trust and understanding with one another. Due to this "connected disconnection" that our global society continues to experience, understanding others and solidifying bonds with them is becoming increasingly difficult.

This doesn't mean that technology is humanity's nemesis; on the contrary, technology is improving global transportation, healthcare, the speed of communication, our response to climate challenges, access to education, and a plethora of other disparities that need attention.

Our challenge lies in the rapid rate at which technology is improving and changing. As humans, we are not equipped to deal with the rapid rate of change we are currently living in. Any new habit or different way of doing things requires time—quite a bit of it—and we are not giving ourselves the time we need to adapt to a new operational tempo.

Think of the challenges that exist when starting a new diet or a new workout routine. These are not relatively big changes, but they require an immense conditioning process as well as discipline to achieve. Compare that process to the way you learn how to manage, interact, and invest in human-to-human relationships that are a culmination of your perspective of the world, others, yourself, and previously lived experiences. There is a big difference in what is required, and the time needed to be successful at it.

This book establishes and explores the seven fundamental layers needed to rekindle old relationships, shape, and contour new ones, and redefine what it means to be valuable to another person at the deepest of levels.

Foreword

Anyone who visits a bookstore or library is quickly impressed by the large amount of shelf space devoted to self-help books that promise to help one's ability to establish positive and long-lasting relationships. As one who highly values the power of positive relationships in my personal *and* professional life, I frequently am left wanting and frustrated after reading a few chapters of these books.

When Dr. Gino Collura invited me to write the foreword for this book, I was humbled and thrilled because he always has impressed me with his passion, expertise, and ability to "connect" with people from all walks of life. If there was ever someone who could provide a roadmap on how to build, maintain and grow healthy relationships, he is the best suited for it. His unique and impactful ability to cut out "fluff" and speak to the heart is unparalleled.

In his fascinating discussion, he intertwines the disciplines of human behavior, psychology, neuroscience, philosophy, health, and other disciplines which provide his discussion with intellectual clarity and research-based information. His discussion focuses on the importance of a person's values and the power of the individual to make a difference in the world through the relationships that are established.

I have been an educator for well over fifty years. I have interacted, hopefully influenced, and guided countless students and teachers to make a better tomorrow for themselves, their peers, and lives they will positively impact. The one constant that exists between all generations I have instructed is their ability to genuinely connect with one another. This is an art and science that requires patience, understanding, and wisdom.

The nurturing of positive personal and professional relationships is hard work and requires commitment. In many ways, establishing and experiencing positive relationships is like planting and tending to a beautiful garden of roses. Attention and commitment begin at the preparation stage and continues with passion throughout the life of the garden. A timeless challenge that stands in front of us is not knowing the exact environment needed to plant the garden or the right approach to manage and sustain the roses. This book is timely and very necessary. With broken relationships, mental health challenges, and consistent division woven into our society, we all need to learn how to reconnect.

You'll not be disappointed you invested your valuable time into the wisdom and roadmap contained within these pages.

Dr. Collura fuses an eclectic perspective that is a direct consequence of him being a successful executive and influencer.

Dr. Dominic "Dick" J. Puglisi
Professor, Stavros Chair &
Director, USF Stavros Center

Introduction

Abraham Lincoln once said, "No man stands so tall as when he stoops to help a child." If I may be so bold as to add to the legendary 16th President of the United States, "A man stands so tall when he stoops to help anyone."

I believe, wholeheartedly that God gave us all gifts, starting with the gift of life as well as each other. The unique gift shared between these two is the existence of time. We waste it like running water from a faucet, yet when it's about to run out, we'd do anything for more. Time is forever fleeting. We can't stop it, control it, or go back to it. We rise to it, eat to it, set our calendars by it, and make future plans around the anticipation of it. It is the single most important thing we have been given; yet people live their entire lives wasting it, particularly amongst each other.

I've spent the majority of my life navigating challenges and adversity, just as you have. From witnessing a beloved family member get shot in the face when I was at the innocent age of eight years old to being the primary care provider for my mother while she endured the fight of her life with cancer to serving as an anti-kidnapping specialist throughout South America for executives who were targets of dangerous guerrilla groups, I have had my fair share of ups and downs. Like you and every other person on this planet, what helped me push through these and so many other trials and tribulations were relationships. The sense of community, support, belonging, and identity found within relationships gave me hope for the possibilities of "what could be" for my life and those in it.

We are living in such a unique time within the history of our world. We have tools at our disposal that seemingly make relationships very easy to facilitate and navigate yet loneliness, depression, anxiety, and failed understandings of ourselves as well as others are more widespread than ever. We were given the incredible gift of communication to foster community as a means of communing (or sharing life). Yet, we have abused and de-valued the gift of communication, mocked the meaning of a healthy and loving community and forgotten the pillars of what it takes to commune with one another.

Throughout my tenure as a college professor of human behavior I worked with countless students from across the globe and found consistent challenges with two things; relatability and authenticity. We all need to appropriately relate to one another while authentically connecting and communicating.

The same challenges have consistently shown themselves through various roles I have occupied as a behavioral scientist, entrepreneur, "C" suite executive, and coach for high performing leaders and influencers across the globe. Regardless of the depth or type of service being provided there is one constant that is a focal point and that is time. Capitalizing it, optimizing it, and understanding how extraordinarily little of it we have. We waste so much time in our own heads trying to filter out constant noise we are presented with on a daily basis that we do not tap into who we really are and who we really want to be. This is depicted by who you choose to relate to and will consume time within your life you can never get back; the question is, are you utilizing time the way you should be to align your life with healthy, positive, and successful relationships?

Those who are around you are witnesses to your existence. Are they witnessing the true and authentic you or the version of you that blends in as a means of conformity and inauthenticity? If the latter, think about how much precious time you are wasting in a life and journey where each second invested can never be retrieved.

My PhD is in Neuroanthropology. It is a specialized discipline within the field of medical anthropology that combines neuroscience, psychology, biocultural anthropology, and sociology. My journey as a neuroanthropologist and behavioral scientist has taught me one important thing; the majority of us have lost the essence of what it means to relate to one another. We have forgotten the spark that fuels our zest for life and the many fruits we were meant to bear through deep-rooted connections with each other.

Every person is beautifully and uniquely made to live a life defined by relationships that positively impact themselves as well as others. Life will undoubtedly bring nonstop stressors, distractions, trials, losses, illnesses, deaths, broken promises, and, at times, straight up misery. But do not let these trials and tribulations cast a perpetual shadow on the greatness you were destined for. You deserve to be happy, you deserve to be fulfilled, and you deserve to experience the gratification that comes with genuinely helping others so they can ultimately help you.

My wish for you with this book is to provide a raw blueprint for joy and happiness with yourself through the many relationships that occupy your life; some relationships will make sense to keep after reading this book while others may not. Some will require a lot more work while others may be just fine as they are. Regardless, this book will clear dust and mud that is hindering the way you view relationships, your role within them, and I'm so glad it fell into your hands. I believe there is a greater purpose for your life, and those who are in it, you may not even know about. This book will help you find it.

Connected Disconnection

We are in a privileged era in the history of humankind, particularly regarding connectivity. Never before could one pick up a phone, and—in mere seconds—not only be speaking to someone across the globe, but actually looking at that person via Apple's FaceTime.

If you were the only person in your town to like a particular thing, chances are, there are groups online that also cater to that very thing. If you were to play a videogame alone and wanted to talk trash or compete against someone else, you can now play online and be suddenly enmeshed with others in real-time while sharing the same make-believe world.

The "do it faster, better, cheaper" mantra of business has accelerated technology in a way that our grandfathers would have never thought possible. Accordingly, there has never been a time before in the history of mankind when it's been easier or quicker to connect with a fellow human being.

I think it's a wonderful thing. After all, we were created to crave connection. When we were infants, we inherently needed nurturing from someone else in order to survive. Connectivity is ingrained in our DNA and we thirst for it. So much so, that the worst inmates in prison are punished with solitary confinement, a denial of any type of interaction or fellowship with another human being.

The problem with the faster, better, cheaper mantra that works so well in the business world is when it becomes the foundational principle for our relationships. What happens when your happiness and self-worth no longer depend on how many people actually call you on your birthday or show up to your party, but by how many followers you have on social media? What happens is Connected Disconnection.

In the world of human behavior, we often talk about Maslow's Hierarchy of Needs, which in essence, are the bare essentials a human being needs for survival. The needs are stacked like a pyramid, with need number one at the bottom to set the foundation, and need number five at the top, which depicts a life well-lived and fulfilled.

Numbers one and two comprise our basic needs:

1. Physiological needs: food, water, warmth, rest
2. Safety needs: security, safety

Numbers three and four are psychological needs:

3. Belonging and love needs: intimate relationships, friends

4. Esteem needs: prestige, feelings of accomplishment.

Number five is what everyone craves, whether they realize it or not.

5. Self-Actualization: achieving one's full potential, including creative activities.

Sadly, billions of people never come close to realizing their full potential. If you were to ask a 21-year-old his or her purpose in life, they would most likely not have an answer. And, if you were to ask that same question of a 65-year-old, he or she most likely would not have an answer, either.

You will never be in anyone's company nearly as much as your own. Your life; your love life, your financial status, your health, your relationships – are all up to you. It is you who will take action or inaction that will dictate your level of happiness and fulfillment.

Therefore, I submit to you this truth: the most important relationship you have is with yourself—period.

Only by truly knowing oneself, can one strive to fulfill his or her purpose.

I wrote this book for many reasons, some of which I'll share here. Too many people don't know their mission in life, and I think that's a travesty. We have generations of people whose self-confidence has been shattered, riddled with thoughts of suicide, cutting, drugs and alcohol, posturing, and living undesirable lives, even for themselves. The narrative of the importance and their reason for being either got lost or was never discovered.

Better, Faster, Cheaper doesn't work with relationships. If you're constantly looking for a better friend or a better relationship, you'll never sufficiently appreciate the one you currently have to put forth the effort to make that one the best it can be. If you're looking to go viral or quickly grow your business and become an instant millionaire, you'll never put in the work that will sustain your enterprise once you do become successful. And if you look for the cheaper version of anything, you'll never find lasting quality.

Marriages are failing at a rate of 40-50%. Business partnerships are failing at an alarming rate of 80%. Better, Faster, Cheaper is not a one-size-fits-all shoe. It works in technology, but not in human connections or for discovering the realization of oneself.

Our society is marred by social separation. We'd rather text or email than be in the present company of someone—and this includes the people we love! Anxiety disorders have people panicked about getting out of a car to meet another human being. They sweat and their hands get clammy as if they have a meeting with Death itself. Businesses are faltering because the owners and employees have put all of their emphasis on transactional relationships with their clients and employees instead of serving them and cultivating a true human connection.

Parents have children who don't want to ever speak to them again, and I'm referring to thirteen-year-olds! Our society is rife with depressed people who suffer from identity crises. People are living double lives: the imperfect, unglamorous ones that they actually live and the perfect ones they are desperate to portray on social media. Everyone throws around the new, hot buzzword: authenticity, but most people aren't bold enough to truly live the lives they'd like to live.

It's time for you to find you. I designed this book for you to know who you are now and who you are destined to become.

Contained in this book are answers you've been searching for, whether you've ever realized you were in search of them or not. Should you clothe yourself in the Seven Layers I share here, it will open the initial doorway to who you are meant to be. I don't believe in magic wands or age-defying elixirs, so you won't find any quick fixes here. What you will find is the road map to discover who you are and how to embrace and boldly live out your purpose.

Nothing can destroy iron except its own rust. Similarly, nothing can destroy you: your joy, your happiness, your goals, and your dreams, except your own mindset and stagnation. If you're ready for a soul-searching, destiny-seeking journey that will shift your mindset and improve your life, turn the page. Your future you awaits.

Layer One:

You

Most Important

The most important relationship you have is with yourself. *Period.*

This nugget of wisdom has been around for centuries. Your understanding of the "hows" and "whys" of your life lays the foundation for the quality and depth of relationships you can have with others (Anton 2015). What does this mean? It means if you do not unveil the truth that defines you as a person, your reason for existence, and the personal constitution that defines you, you will not be able to sustainably relate to and connect with others. Not giving yourself permission to do this is a travesty as you are leaving so much untouched on the table that is life and robbing yourself of special moments, understandings, and connections you deserve to experience.

For many of us, this is puzzling. We feel confident in who we are, and the culmination of experiences we've lived are combined with aspirations we have yet to achieve. But we fail to realize that there are missing factors and opportunity costs we have paid little mind to; they weren't perceived as priorities because modern culture does not value them as such.

This doesn't mean that choices and decisions were made with the intention of separating us from our truth. On the contrary, we often chase a version of ourselves that we think we need to be, believing that doing so will fulfill one of the many voids we experience within the journey of our life's course. This is a byproduct of the influence our social and institutional structures have upon our lives which are woven into our perception of the world. The right education vs. the wrong education, the right career vs. a temporary job, the successful lifestyle vs. being poverty-stricken, and so on—all things that are tied to our initial framings (perceptions) and blueprints of the world.

An example of framing is something as simple as a conversation with a good friend. My understanding of that person, their emotions, their temperament, their expectations (as well as mine) establishes the framing of that interaction. It applies to anything and everything that guides expected outcomes. We are not conditioned to challenge our framing as it goes against the grain of the institutions that instilled them (schools, government, family, friends, social groups, commerce, religion, etc.) and is often perceived as dangerous or haphazard to do so. This can facilitate personal blind spots that have a lingering influence on everything we do and can cause internal pressure we don't recognize and often cast aside. This forfeits our recognition of important identity pillars that influence our ability to authentically connect with others.

True connection requires at least two sources that are in sync; how can you be in sync with someone else if you are not in sync with yourself?

Pressure Source

Think of the pressure you feel at any given time. Why is it there? Pressure is one of the greatest tools that crafts, shapes and molds us into different versions of ourselves throughout our life. Ponder every great event that has happened in your life. What role did pressure play? What about catastrophic events? What role did it play? Identifying internal drivers and where they come from is what I call your "pressure source." This concept is *ingredient number one* to understanding your "whys." Recognizing them allows us to see influences that have brought us to our lived conclusions, or at least the way we perceive and make sense of our experiences.

The tough part is the "making sense" side of it; this is where bias lives due to deprivations you have experienced throughout your life, deprivations that drive the "meaning making" process, which differs from one person to the next.

Consider a life goal you have and answer the question, "Why do I have this goal?" Something, somewhere in the journey that is your life attached significance to what achieving that goal would mean. It fills a void that was created along the way and generates tentacles of associative pressure that drive you to complete the goal. For example, I have not met one fellow PhD who did not experience some level of deprivation that created an obsession with their chosen field of expertise. The same applies for MDs or any other rigorous educational, physical, or professional endeavor where countless hours and sacrifice are required to fill a void through accomplishing a goal.

Our challenge is that we get caught up in the vision of the goal instead of what drove us to it in the first place; hence, once the goal is complete, we carry blind spots and experience temporary satisfaction rather than sustainable fulfillment. We get addicted to the feeling of "what could be" and "what it will be like" (which is but a temporary satisfaction of the existing void) and this feeling masks the pressure points that drive the creation of those end results.

When it comes to life changes, our brain has a difficult time making "the harder choice" (Anton 2015). It enjoys sensations that provide constant dopamine, serotonin, oxytocin, and endorphin releases (our feel good/happy neurohormones) associated with what the end result will be and what we think it will mean to us when we get there. *The truth of your authentic nature is not found in the end result; it is defined by the curves, peaks and valleys you lean into that forge your identity along the way.* Those moments of pressure change the essence of your being that define the little wins and losses you endure every day. This is really good stuff, so pay attention to it as it is what you need to immerse yourself in and understand.

Pressure perceived is change to be achieved. That lived change is what alters the level of pressure you will continue to experience, or perhaps not. *The more comfortable you are with change, the less pressure you will feel.* Once you understand "pressure sources," you can apply that understanding to your identity alignment, and this is where the magic really happens! But getting yourself aligned is tough. It is a struggle between personal desires, social pressures, and the expectations we have of ourselves and others, which often clash. It runs parallel with achieving balance in your life; it is a constant journey toward something that can often feel impossible to achieve as there is no final destination, and there never will be.

The goal here is to understand what optimal alignment looks like. We all have an understanding of *who* we are; but *how* we align ourselves with our purpose, others, goals, and manage disappointment/pain yet to come (and previously lived) shines a different light on what future versions of ourselves could be. Knowing and recognizing this begins with identifying gaps between personal domains that define our existence and impact our relationships.

Think of it this way: how many different hats do you wear as a human being? Meaning, how many roles do you play and what do those roles mean to you? All of us can say that we are a son/daughter, some of us can say that we are a parent, sibling, athlete, leader, employee, business owner, student, and the list goes on and on. The majority of us tend to shift our behavior, communication pattern, vernacular, tonality, and energy depending on what hat we are wearing. This falls in line with the well-known *chameleon effect* that is discussed in behavioral and psychological domains (Chartrand & Bargh 1999). It establishes the idea that we make temporary real-time adaptations to blend in better with others with whom we seek to grow relationships.

If the shifts in behavior contribute to your growth as a human being, this is a good thing as it makes the "harder choice" easier to accomplish. If they are behaviors that *do not* contribute to your growth and development yet have been justified as a means of getting you closer to an established goal or disparity that you are seeking to fill, you could be entering a danger zone. *Be careful about silently picking up traits and characteristics that do not align with your core values.*

This is a silent trap that causes "cracks in the foundation of our core." So many of us do not know the vulnerabilities associated with our inner selves because we do not know what our core is made of. This takes us back to pressure sources. Knowing what invokes pressure shines light on what we are made of, as well as what we are not made of.

Cracks present opportunities for both growth and destruction. Think of it this way: when you go to the gym and try a new exercise, you are working muscles in a new way. Undoubtedly, you are going to feel sore for a day or two after you exercise as you have created micro-tears within your muscle tissue. With rest, water, and the right nutrients, your muscle will recover and become stronger than it was before you performed the exercise. But, if you do not provide rest, water, and the right nutrients, you run the possibility of those micro-tears turning into a large tear when that muscle is exerted. The same principle applies to the cracks in our foundation.

When we form cracks to make ourselves better, this is a good thing because we are making the harder choice to create new neuropathways and develop a better understanding of our complete potential. As we push ourselves to greater lengths toward achieving our goals and rising to meet the expectations we've set for ourselves, we invite growth. When this is done with the right outlook and process, it can be rewarding. But, when this is done haphazardly or simply for the sake of doing it to blend in, we make our authenticity factor vulnerable to cracks that can push us farther away from our truth that can break us. We create a wilderness with pitfalls and traps that can lead us down roads that push us farther away from being the best version of ourselves.

In John Maxwell's world-renowned book, "The 21 Irrefutable Laws of Leadership," he discusses the importance of adding value to others. He titles this "Law #5: The Law of Addition." Maxwell makes a compelling case for listening and learning before leading others as well as before choosing to follow others. When you choose to alter and change as a means of conforming, be sure that the individuals you are conforming to align with your authentic nature and the life you want to have.

If they don't, prepare yourself for a temporary and unfulfilling relationship. Be cautious with how much you invest in such relationships because 99% of the time they will not stand the test of time; they will eventually push you to a place you won't like. The process could take months, years, or even decades, but eventually that conformity is going to gnaw at the essence of your identity as that misalignment of values will not hold up to future pressure sources you will experience.

Who You Belong With

Recognizing which relationships fit and which ones don't requires clarity and truth within ourselves. We must be honest about what makes us authentically happy and why. We must be naked about our fears and our worries as well as our doubts and face them head-on. We cannot put bandages over emotional and psychological scars we endured in childhood, adolescence, and adulthood. We need extreme ownership of these experiences and the impact they have on our world and self-view. This is the only way to reach our full potential as individuals as well as within relationships.

If you are of the mindset that honesty about who you are is contingent upon what others say about you or how they perceive you, then that is exactly where we need to start.

At any given time, other individuals are only seeing a piece of the total that is you. Allowing their perception and opinion to sway the pillars that define you indicates instability within your self-understanding and what you value within. Maintaining humility while being boldly confident in who you are is where the good stuff is. The key words here are humility and confidence, not cockiness or narcissism. *Owning your lived experiences leads to self-accountability, and that is the most difficult, yet important form of accountability.*

But let's take a big spoonful of truth: *you lie to yourself every day—we all do.* We paint a façade of who we are and where we are in the journey of life and the relationships we have with others.

How does it make any sense to lie to ourselves on a regular basis? Why do we do it?

We do it to make sense. We do it to reduce ambiguity (which, within our brains, translates to danger). We do it to feel at ease with the choices and investments we have made with the most important commodity that any one of us has: time.

The challenge is that we intentionally believe the lies we tell ourselves because they make us feel comfortable and feed mental models (Senge 1990) that go unchallenged. This perpetuates a cycle of inauthenticity that we become blind to and creates assumptions and understandings of ourselves that are not accurate.

Your truth is found in challenging your way of doing things and piecing apart the way you think and feel so you can unveil the models that are working within. Without understanding those models, you are simply going through static motions that limit growth, understanding, and possibilities for the best version of yourself.

Objectivity and Decision Making

It's hard for us to be honest with ourselves, let alone with others. So many of us don't want to because it often contradicts with the version of ourselves that we'd like to think we currently are or that others perceive. So, we have this hurdle that consists of our ego as well as the coping mechanisms we use, mechanisms that serve solely as bandages for wounds that require sutures and surgical precision to fully heal and understand. How do you overcome such a hurdle? It starts with grasping objectivity with your decision-making habits, your initial reactions to things, as well as the marriage that exists between your emotions and your logic. If you are not able to clearly understand each one of these, it's because you don't know what you're looking for, which in turn *tells* you what to look for. So, let's start with objectivity.

Gaining objectivity is a difficult task that most of us are not willing to undertake because we don't understand the rewards for personal growth that come along with it. Anyone who has spent time in the fields of human behavior or psychological research understands the importance of analyzing, interpreting, and reporting research data as objectively as possible. This is done so that data is not skewed, tainted, or misrepresented due to special interests, emotional compromise, or other hopeful outcomes. The data must be exactly what it is: factual.

How do we achieve legitimate objectivity when we are emotionally vested in others as well as ourselves? There is no secret sauce here. Reaching objectivity requires the skillset of removing our own compromises before they influence our perspective on a person or a situation.

This is hard, really hard, which is why it requires practice and accountability. Fostering the discipline to keep your emotions and views in check requires you to know *exactly* what your views and beliefs are. Without having a confident understanding of those elements, you will fail to achieve objectivity within your decision-making and relationship management ability.

A great activity that can help kickstart this process is crafting your own personal constitution, a living, breathing document that outlines everything you believe in and feel you represent. Write it out. Study it. Ask those closest to you if that is how they believe you are. Then, continue to question everything about it. Why do you believe the things you do? Why will you not tolerate certain things in your life? What events and failed relationships have transpired within your life to craft your constitution in that particular way? These are all healthy and exploratory questions that contribute to the even bigger questions of who you are. Here is a brief excerpt from mine that may help you get started:

> *I, Gino Collura, as a means of fulfilling my existence with meaning, impact, positive influence, and good deeds, establish this constitution to serve as my North Star throughout the duration of my life.*
>
> *My personal relationships mean everything to me as they define the roots of where I come from. It is my duty and obligation to be loyal to my parents, wife, daughter, select extended family, and friends who I consider family. Their investment in me is the greatest gift I could ever receive, and I will honor them through my very last breath on this earth.*
>
> *I will honor myself and the gifts I have been given. I am a builder, protector, and influencer of fellow men and women. I have been given the gift of wisdom, insight, and charisma that allows me to speak to the body, mind, and spirit of my peers. I will honor these gifts through serving others with integrity, honesty, and commitment to help them in their journey of becoming who they are destined to be.*
>
> *My existence was predetermined. I am not a byproduct of time, matter, or chance. I was designed with a specific purpose to help my fellow man throughout this journey*

of life. My guidance and influence should always come directly from God and no one or nowhere else. I believe in truth. I believe in love. I believe in temperance. I believe in justice. I believe in discipline. I believe in grace."

When was the last time you defined *you* to yourself? I'm not talking about your name, your profession, your social or your familial roles, I'm talking about the *you* that is your purpose. The *you* that is your life source and pumps blood through your veins and prompts you to keep putting one foot in front of the other. The *you* that undeniably defines your existence and will leave a mark when you are no longer walking this earth. Most of us have absolutely *no idea*.

Hard Truth

The truth is that the majority of us are not willing to challenge our established "normal." We don't want to break our standardized perceptions of viewing the world and make choices that lead to deeper understanding and relationship improvements; this process challenges the framework of established neurocircuitry that has done its job in creating a sense of "how it's supposed to be" and the anticipated reactions that follow. Pushing against our playbook means work, and lots of it, with a dive into the unknown that our brain interprets as danger. The only reason why it's considered "dangerous" is because it's unknown. Once it becomes known, it has the potential to become a new normal.

This brings us full circle to the "cracks in our core" and the opportunity we have at our fingertips when we foster intentional ambiguity. With ambiguity, we can create opportunities that further weaken us or take the opportunity of having cracks that fortify us and become stronger than ever. *Managing the ambiguity starts with assuming objectivity of ourselves so that we can identify the blind spots that we generally pay no mind to.* Once they're properly identified, we can get to work.

This approach falls in line with professional support groups across the country, the mantra of "the first step in recovering from an issue is recognizing that you have an issue", honesty with yourself is the same exact thing. *You cannot begin to uncover a deeper understanding of your wants and needs unless you understand why your wants and needs exist in the first place.* Those wants and needs represent blueprints that have been set and defined by lived moments in your childhood/adolescence (for most of us) and exciting/traumatic experiences throughout adulthood. What assigns the level of influence they have at a subconscious and conscious level is what you have made them mean to you.

When looking through the halls of history, you will find that almost every advanced society, philosopher, and poet had thoughts on the value of "meaning making" and understanding your objective truth; René Descartes and his Cartesian theory, John Locke and his critique of Cartesian theory, David Hume's Bundle Theory, Fyodor Dostoevsky's depictions of psychosocial dynamics (as seen in *"The Double")*, and Mencius with his writings on human nature among thousands of other great thinkers. Recognizing that you need a greater understanding of yourself is a difficult thing to grasp, particularly once you hit your thirties, forties, fifties and beyond because after a few decades of walking the planet, so many of us think we know ourselves. The truth is, we don't.

Reactions

What exactly is a reaction? It's the *how* in your response to the interpretation of stimuli.

Fun fact: Your brain produces 12,000–60,000 thoughts a day. Where do those thoughts stem from? What sorts of stimuli are conjuring neurons for us to interpret and respond to? Our understood reality is based upon constant stimuli that forces us to react as well as make sense of the actions, thoughts, and emotions we experience daily. This means that we're making thousands of decisions every single day, which is why our brains create shortcuts. Unfortunately, those shortcuts slowly build gaps in our ability to be objective and consider all perspectives because they are based on efficiency and not mindfulness of another's perspective or actions.

We should strive to unwind many of these gaps as a means of recognizing exactly what they are, which stems from our understanding of life, relationships, purpose, and meaning that is created from our individual journey.

When was the last time you defined your personal story?

Is it where you come from? Is it your family? Is it your friends? Is it the things you like and don't like? Being honest with yourself means being honest about why you do what you do and understanding why. For example, let's say you have an immense drive to be successful and avoid failure. Where does *that* stem from? You have a constant need for praise and affirmation, what does that drive you to do? We often mask our story in "That's just how I am," with zero regard for how we could be better if we were willing to push the bounds of normalcy that we confine ourselves to. Normalcy equates to comfort, and comfort means easy.

That's exactly what your brain wants: easy. Since you burn minimal calories when you aren't firing neurons and creating new neuropathways, *easy* is the fundamental pillar of self-preservation. Just like any good personal trainer will tell you, the key to success with physical fitness is constantly challenging your body to perform in ways you didn't think it could. The same is true for your brain. *Finding comfort in the uncomfortable is a necessary ingredient to achieving regular neurogenesis (the creation of new neurons) which everyone is capable of throughout the entire course of their life.*

This is vital when capturing the true potential of our individuality and separating ourselves from our peers while also discovering why we stagnate in our understanding of ourselves, which contributes to the quality and depth of interaction we have with others (Anton 2015).

Layer Two:
Your Source

Belief

This is one of the most powerful words that exists in the English language. As a concept, it has immense force and influence and has achievable outcomes attached, outcomes that have propelled motivation in human beings since the beginning of time. From the creation of the light bulb to landing on the moon, being confident in our beliefs comes from knowing and understanding our truths and what we stand for as human beings.

This is where cross-cultural interactions really come to life as many different groups, classes, and cultures carry varied understandings and interpretations of self-purpose depending on what they were taught by preceding generations as well as what they endured during their life experiences. Since emotional influence is often compromised by the unexpected nature of lived experiences, these ebbs and flows of life conjure an ever-changing kaleidoscope of perspectives that are sometimes difficult to make sense of. These ambiguous moments only center themselves to our identity when the belief we carry of our purpose and principles makes sense.

Due to the ever-changing nature of access to data (internet, social media, TV, etc.), societal expectations as well as "normal" social interactions, so many young and old minds no longer know what to believe in. This is a problem. *To discern the importance of their existence and what they believe their life amounts to, human beings need a concrete compass.* In a time where every single perspective is rationalized, we have paid a huge price for not having a clear understanding of what is acceptable, what defines us as a culture, and the importance of having shared principles.

Some of the greatest minds to have walked this earth have taken a stab at understanding belief's etymology, purpose, and pliability amongst different groups across the world. Plato, St. Augustine, Aristotle, and many others, have dissected and explored belief, why it is so important within the human condition, and how it aids in creating rapport, bonds, and meaningful relationships. For most, belief is something relatively simple to encapsulate. It represents things you think to be true that contribute to the way you see the world and how you judge what is good, bad, acceptable, and not acceptable. The key phrase here is "think to be true."

How we come to conclusions of what the truth actually is has everything to do with the depth of understanding of that perceived truth in the first place. This is where knowing your *why* is important as well as breaking molds and barriers which have formed *closed loops* instead of *open loops* within your neurocircuitry that can lead to greater adaptability and understanding. This means that you're willing to push the boundaries and understandings within your brain and search inside yourself to recognize and engage other ways of thinking about the truth and what it actually means to you and your identity.

Contrary to what modern psychology professes, beliefs are simply not "energy-saving shortcuts in modeling and predicting one's environment" (Lewis 2018), they are much more than that as they require us to take a good look at why we do the things we do and how it is that our peers perceive the value we bring to the table throughout relationships. Consider this, have you ever explored the reason for your physical existence?

It's a daunting question indeed.

Where *did* you come from, and why *are* you here? Do you believe that you're a byproduct of millions of years of evolution? Do you believe that your great ancestors were brought here by an extraterrestrial life form? Do you believe that you were created in the image of a deity and endowed with specific talents and abilities to carry out a particular path in life? Do you believe that you are a culmination of previous lives that connect you to ancestors who may now be represented in different life forms (bugs, animals, fish, etc.)? These are big questions, and they matter. Popular culture preaches that such big questions are not worth exploration; rather, the latest social media campaign or TV dramas are seen as better uses for your time. This is a problem.

If you don't have a belief in your *why,* nor how you came to be, then your perceived beliefs are always shifting which means you're constantly changing the value of your existence. Does this mean that changing your beliefs is bad? Not at all. That's part of maturing the many lenses that make up your perception of the world and lived experiences that influence different perspectives at any given time. *What matters are the roots that anchor your value system and how well you understand them.*

These beliefs are not simply based on rationalization such that they could easily be influenced by a clever argument. These beliefs are absolutes, beliefs that ignite your inner spark and create relentless focus, drive, and commitment. These are things that, due to societal demands that are rooted in a shallow understanding of our purpose, many of us have turned a blind eye to. Such demands, fueled by technology, make self-discovery nearly impossible since artificial intelligence now does the "discovering" at the push of a button. Incredible learning and growth are thus excised from the self-discovery journey, simultaneously fostering a co-dependence upon answers pertaining to our identity. This dependence has deafened our ability to not only listen to our inner voice, but to also question where that inner voice comes from.

Possessing the belief that we are attached to (or part of) something greater than ourselves makes our lives mean more, and at the end of the day, meaning really matters.

Take an inventory of what is meaningful in your life. What does it mean to love someone? What does it mean to sacrifice for your children or others? What does it mean to put your life on the line for someone else? When you believe your existence is part of something greater than yourself, these questions become easy to answer; yet, how many lines of thinking dominate your perceptions and solely assign meaning to make you feel good in a particular moment, perpetuating egocentric or self-centered behavior?

When you believe that your existence is simply your existence, nothing more and nothing less, this is the resulting challenge. When we become fixated on the notion that all we must live for is ourselves, with no belief that our actions contribute to a culmination of behavior attached to something else, it becomes incredibly easy to get caught up in a vicious cycle of narcissistic or self-absorbed behavior.

For example, I am a Christian. I wholeheartedly believe that Jesus Christ was real and that he set an example of how God wants us to live. Along with my belief, I recognize, appreciate, and regularly learn from others who carry different understandings than I do whether they are a Christian of a different denomination, or whether they're Muslim, Jewish, Hindu, Buddhist, Sikh, or of any other belief system that attaches meaning and purpose to existence.

Where challenges present themselves is when the value and purpose of life becomes undermined through fads and cultural conditioning patterns found in most social institutions across the country.

I have been fortunate to receive an incredible education in human behavior, human history, and the projected trends of human interactions in the decades/centuries to come. This education came with a clear understanding of scientific processes, quantitative and qualitative data inquiry, the nature of insider vs. outsider perspectives, applied neuroscience, as well as appropriate methods for participant observation that minimizes bias as much as possible, and it was fantastic.

But my thirteen-year journey throughout the social institution that is higher education did not come without compromise. On more occasions than I can remember, I verbally grappled with colleagues over ideologies and perspectives on what it means to be a human being. I don't discredit this experience; on the contrary, I'm thankful for it as that is what higher education is supposed to be about. But it unveiled a quickness to poke holes or make fun of belief systems that find purpose in a "bigger than me" perspective.

This is problematic, and it is indicative of the level of intolerance and depths of "cancel culture" we are seeing run rampant throughout every echelon of society, as well as influential institutions throughout our country. This matters because of the shaping and contouring it is doing to young minds and the impact it will have for upcoming generations.

Individuals who are occupying roles in management, leadership, and influence are not becoming equipped with the appropriate tools and skills to understand the necessity of active belief in a greater purpose. They are constantly finding themselves bombarded with one thing after another and therefore, do not give themselves the time to cultivate an understanding of who they are (introspectively) without the demands and influence of pop culture. Their identity has become a question of productivity and "getting things done" instead of fulfilling and serving their life's calling attached to something bigger than themselves. This greatly influences the quality of leadership and influence they can provide.

Since purpose and meaning really matter, why would we choose to believe in a meaningless life? Let's briefly examine the atheist perspective and dive into some challenges that present themselves (no disrespect to any atheists reading this—this is simply an observation). According to atheistic logic on evolution, our existence stems from three tenets: time, matter, and chance. Time, being how we measure the length of existence; matter, being things traveling and existing throughout time; and chance, being things that occur without intention, cause or understanding.

So, let's combine those. We know that time is always changing, matter is always shifting, and chance is nothing more than an assignment to a happening that we cannot understand or clearly define (Zacharias 2004). The culmination of all three is what created your brain and our existence as a species. Now, think about that.

If this were the case, what role does *purpose* play? What role does *how we treat others* play? Do *they* even matter? If we are nothing more than a byproduct of time, matter, and chance, and these are always shifting, how can we ever find absolute meaning in our existence? The short answer is that we cannot.

Here is a different perspective. What is the distinction between confronting a teenage shoplifter or facing down a forty-year-old serial rapist? I believe most of us would say that there is a big difference between both transgressors; yet, if we are simply organisms that are a byproduct of time, matter, and chance, then where does the evaluation that one act is worse than the other stem from?

A jurisprudence argument could be made that legal and moral standards are one and the same, signifying that there is something much bigger at play than simply time, matter, and chance. If this were true, then why do we care about the transgressions that others make against us or people we identify with? Why do we care or get a gut feeling that something isn't right? If it is for the sole purpose to keep us alive and away from danger, then what is the point as our existence has no meaning because we are simply organisms that were created as a byproduct of time, matter, and chance.

Time only has assigned meaning because it's a construct. Matter has no emotion and chance has no significance as nothing (which Aristotle defined as "that which rocks dream about") can materialize from it, yet they are the things that created us, so where is our purpose found (Zacharias 2004)? This is the challenge we face in our current era. Rationalizing things that have no meaning while we find a way to conjure meaning with no understanding as to why.

Having faith and commitment to the source that created your roots perpetuates deeper meaning and understanding, providing guidelines and a purpose for life we all feel a connection to. For example, if you believe that your existence is nothing more than a stroke of luck within the universe, then what role do good and evil play? If there is no meaning assigned to your existence, then what difference does your existence make? How can you conjure the confidence to identify the motivation and what fuels it in the first place if there is no meaning that stems from belief?

Look to the halls of history and think about some of the most heinous atrocities that have ever transpired. Hitler and his orchestration of the Holocaust, the Rwandan Genocide of 1994, the Nanjing Massacre of 1937, the September 11th attacks and a litany of other events that have been deemed evil, atrocious, and violations of fundamental human rights. If we were not connected to something much bigger than simply time, matter, and chance, these sorts of events would not matter to us because our purpose and meaning would be arbitrary and have no deeper meaning.

As a species, we can feel that it is simply not the case. There is an abundance of evidence that shows we are connected to something bigger than ourselves, a collective consciousness that provides meaning and purpose that make us different than any other species on the planet.

Decisions Matter, But What Are They Based Upon?

We choose what we think about and what we think about becomes the basis for decisions we make within our lives. As Lao Tzu said, "Watch your thoughts, they become your words; watch your words, they become your actions; watch your actions, they become your habits; watch your habits, they become your character; watch your character, it becomes your destiny."

Our decisions are a culmination of considerations that we experience daily and contain patterns of association to cyclical life development. Considering past experiences, socioeconomics, emotional temperance, education, self-awareness, societal structures, and cultural hegemony are vital when comprehending different influences on our decision-making abilities within the life cycle.

Cultural hegemony was developed by Marxist intellectual, Antonio Gramsci, to describe the domination of popular culture by the ruling class as a means of establishing constructed societal norms with regards to beliefs, values, and perceptions.

Historically, anthropological and biological investigations have shed immense light on how modern-day human beings make decisions (Neugarten 1979). Taking close examination of the stages within human evolution, modern-day Homo Sapiens indicate that there have been clear developmental shifts in societal and relationship complexity over time. Being in a hunter-gatherer society is vastly different from being in a technologically advanced society where we choose what we want to eat, control our climate, find solace in all our necessities being met and have time to not worry about being eaten by a Tyrannosaurus Rex.

Lingering throughout each one of these stages has been an important thread that contoured and shaped the continuum of life experience to the creation of the genus Homo: the role of biotic (other living beings) and abiotic (environmental) selective pressures that have influenced the value and purpose of hominid relationships pertaining to survival, contentment, and prosperity as a species.

When observing the twelve stages of the life cycle as taught by Dr. Thomas Armstrong of the American Institute for Learning and Human Development, each stage predicates the other and contributes to the collective consciousness established within macro cultures and shapes the decision-making process within cultures and the relationships that compose them.

Life Cycle Stages:

1. Prebirth
2. Birth
3. Infancy (Ages 0-3)
4. Early Childhood (Ages 3-6)
5. Middle Childhood (Ages 6-8)
6. Late Childhood (Ages 9-11)
7. Adolescence (Ages 12-20)
8. Early Adulthood (Ages 20-35)
9. Midlife (Ages 35-50)
10. Mature Adulthood (Ages 50-80)
11. Late Adulthood (Age 80+)
12. Death and Dying

Priorities shift within and between each stage that alter how we make decisions for ourselves as well as others. An often-overlooked aspect within the decision-making process are the biological consequences associated with them.

Take into consideration the biocultural synthesis as proposed and applied by Dr. Alan Goodman and Dr. Thomas Leatherman in 1998. Their studies involving real-time biological changes that are a direct result of cultural norms and practices shed light on various influences that have an outcome tied to daily decision making and understanding of what one's purpose is. You know just as well as I do that the "meaning making" process shifts throughout the life cycle; things such as maturity, lived experiences, and our interpretation of varying social norms will change depending on our personal hierarchy of needs that influence how we make things and others mean something to us (Tierney 2018).

A good example of this can be seen within the military population who actively engage in combat. Studies have shown that repetitive conditioning of a combative culture has very real biological consequences at a physical and microbiological level (Collura & Lende 2012). Changes in the hypothalamus, pituitary, and adrenal gland function (stress response system) have a direct impact on how combatants manage stress and can affect their decision-making abilities and who they are able to relate to.

Combine that line of thought with other life-cycle factors, such as experiencing bullying in childhood, confusion of social norms within adolescence, repetitive heartbreak, political beliefs in young adulthood and the growing political hostility we all have become privy to, and we can see where cultural factors become internalized and have real biological consequences (poor mental health, a compromised immune system, neurohormonal imbalances, etc.).

In a study of New York City mothers who were pregnant during the September 11th attacks, data was highlighted that associated the heightened level of stress to low birth rates and an increase in miscarriages as well as stress disorders within the newborn population (Engel et al. 2015). Epigenetically, this makes sense. Something that challenged our survivability as a culture generated enough stress to cause biological challenges that had a negative outcome. We forget that throughout life, we are dealing with a constant bombardment of stressors that take their toll on our understanding of the world, how we identify ourselves within it, as well as the value of the exchange and interchange we have with others.

This fortifies the need for us to have clarity on exactly what our lives mean while bringing us full circle as to why this is so important. It's a question of optimizing your quality of life and the quality of life of those you surround yourself with. If you believe that you're nothing more than a consequence of matter, time, and chance, then why do any of the above examples matter? You're simply a biological petri dish with a specific genetic code made of bacteria and microbes that are remnants of stardust and natural elements.

What role do meaning, purpose, or internal depth play in any of that? If there is no morality and there's no significance tied to your existence, then why do your peace, your time, or the quality of your life and relationships with others matter? Technically, meaning has nothing to do with time, matter, or chance but we all know that it does. It matters because you were designed with purpose and intent, and you belong to something much bigger than yourself: *your identity is that you are a piece of humanity, and mankind is incredibly special and unique.*

We have complex communication, the ability to describe to one another what it is we feel and think, education systems that allow us to archive and study history, the skills to invent and create new things to make future generations live a different type of life, as well as many other capacities that separate us from other mammals and the animal kingdom at large.

Something, somewhere along the continuum of time caused our design and intent to become inherently different than other living creatures on this earth, and you must discover what that means to you. You must look to your inner core and unveil your source so that you can live a life that is anchored deeply in the truth of who you are and where you come from. Only then will you be able to begin the journey of connecting to others as your authentic self.

GINO L. COLLURA

Battling Moral Decay

As a species, we have been in search for greater meaning in our existence and purpose for thousands of years. Ever since we found dependable food sources, consistent shelter, and the opportunity for community where we could exchange ideas, we have openly fostered the will to explore significance, meaning, context, and enhanced intelligence. With millennia of this exchange well under our belts, we have found every possible way to dissect, organize, exploit, and manipulate ways of thinking about ourselves and one another.

The Axial age (8th to 3rd Century BCE) brought us the fundamentals of Confucianism, the Classic period brought us Platonism and the Cynics, the Post-Classical period brought us Christianity and its many schisms as well as the Renaissance, with its eventual dive into Modernism, the Scientific Revolution, Rationalism, the Enlightenment, Post-Modernism, and now Post-Millennialism. Each of these historical periods brought an array of notable thinkers, texts, and belief systems, but the part to really grasp is that human beings thirst for answers and knowledge because we have an incredible capacity to systematically investigate (and attempt to make sense of) numerous things. Our challenge is that, in our quest for answers, we undermine the big picture of what it is we're attempting to make sense of. In other words, *our search for meaning has downplayed the significance of what we seek to create meaning for.*

Along the way, we got caught up in holes that become obsessions. We no longer search for objective truth; now we're only concerned with "our truth," thinking that such a truth applies as a universal constant, when in reality, our own rationalization (which is defined solely by our individual knowledge, experience, emotional regulation, and aptitude for objectivity) is constantly shifting as "new" data gets filtered and applied. We live in an unprecedented era that pressures us to keep a daily operational tempo that our brains were not designed for. This has manifested itself through increased cases of mental illness, substance addiction, broken relationships, political dismay, division among families and groups, as well as the societal discord we are all well aware of.

We're expected to have an answer (or at least a response) at all times without valuing solitude and self-reflection. We preach "mindfulness" without knowing what it means to be mindful or how to achieve it. We're encouraged to obsess over news, sports, social media, and TV dramas rather than introspectively analyzing our thoughts and how they impact those we seek to have relationships with. *Our culture has become nothing more than an imitation of data that is fed into objects and tools that we are told are necessary (cell phones/*

computers/tablets/TVs) but represent nothing more than a luxury.

We've become lost within a sense of comfort that has rendered us idle, unable to dig into the inner depths of our being, the place where truth lies. This is the decay that has come to contemporary human relations. *We simply have too much time, yet still not enough. Too much time becomes dedicated to things that frame our thoughts, expectations, and emotions, and not enough time is devoted to the framing of what our lives mean based on objective, introspective reflection.*

What makes you valuable in a relationship? How do you justify to yourself which relationships are worthwhile and which ones are not? Most of us don't know how to measure our value, let alone the significance of someone else we share a relationship with. How can we ever understand others if we can't understand the value of ourselves? How can you know the value of yourself if you don't know the value of your own existence? How can you know the value of your existence if you don't know where you come from and why?

This brings us back to the second layer of knowing your source. You must have a North Star and something that justifies why you're worthy of a relationship with those you desire to relate with. You need something that fuels belief in yourself and others that makes the time spent with one another worthwhile rather than simply "something you do" because society says it's normal.

Our capacity to love one another, to care and sacrifice for one another, to exchange and share ideas is predicated upon how well we can serve each other. Since, due to technological advancements in our society, ease of accessibility and comfort are the things we've become conditioned for, we get hung up on self-service and continuously do things that feel good, right and comfortable. Without responsible use, these comforts bring compromises that distract us from finding our source.

LAYER THREE:

Alignment

Independent Understanding

In the early stages of life, we are indoctrinated with a clear understanding of what we need to survive: proper shelter, water, food, climate, etc. All of these are staple pillars to live on this earth, and this is reflected in the well-known Maslow's Hierarchy of Needs:

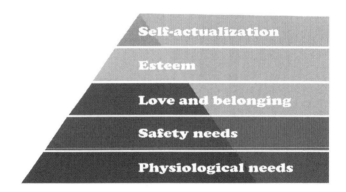

Once these basic physiological needs are met, there follows a shift to safety, love and belonging, esteem, and eventually, self-actualization. These layers build upon one another and are dependent upon interactions with others. That is how we have become the dominant species on this planet, through our ability to work synergistically with others to achieve milestones and goals that mean something to improve our quality of life.

Understanding the importance of dependency is vital in achieving an independent understanding of where you belong and why.

Simply stated, our species would be long extinct had it not been for our capacity to trust one another and highlight the value that "the other" has in our lives. This defines the human essence and our capacity to live in service to each other. *We don't often think about the importance of dependence in our everyday lives because that would generate a feeling of vulnerability that would challenge our sense of independence.* Yet, if we really break down each stage of Maslow's Hierarchy of Needs, even the most basic of needs are predicated on the existence of us having dependence on one another.

Think of it this way: when a child is born, it is completely incapable of providing for itself. It relies on Mom/Dad/guardian to provide food, shelter, a suitable environment, protection from predators, etc., and that is in the very first phase of needs that must be met for it to move up the hierarchy.

Dependency never leaves us, especially in modern times. We depend on grocery stores, managed and constructed by others, for food. The security for our home is provided by alarm systems which are monitored by others. We rely upon others for employment, or else we engage in providing services to others in exchange for our own livelihood. Others provide reinforcement of our own identity and worth in the intimate relationships we share. The list goes on and on. *We are completely dependent upon one another, not only for our survival, but also in how we identify where we belong and who we belong with.* This identification process is a culmination of the first two layers of successful relationships (knowing yourself as well as your source) and is often challenged by our ability to properly align ourselves with others, as that can become complicated.

Subjectively understanding who we are and objectively knowing what is best for us creates conflict as the subjective is a specific lens we are looking through on any given day, which is subject to change because our moods and perceptions frequently change. Others around us have an impact on how we manage our day as well as how we feel about ourselves. One of the largest fallacies is that we shouldn't care what others think about us. Now, in theory, it makes sense. Building a wall that deafens the words and opinions of others that could be offensive or hurtful is a protective mechanism that keeps us focused and in a clear state. But is that attainable? And, even if it is, is it sustainable?

I believe we all get to a point in our own depth and understanding where it becomes a possibility but requires a grounded confidence of the objective vs. subjective sides of ourselves. With dependence woven into the fabric of being human, we look to others for self-validation, support, and examples of how things should be done. This all comes with a measurement of how we stack up in relation to our peers to identify where it is we belong and what the right fit for us should be. Imagine attaining this type of authentic understanding without having the first two layers established and understood. You can't.

So many of us don't know what our true identity is. We haven't gone through the introspective abyss of our inner selves to know our purpose, which dictates the people we should surround ourselves with, the types of relationships we should nurture, and the outcomes those relationships will have on our growing self-understanding. Most of us experience alignment with others as a direct byproduct of comfort and complacency. We align ourselves for the easier things in life (low-hanging fruit) because that's the least amount of work and our brains like that. Your brain does not like having to forge new neuropathways; it's difficult, frustrating, and cumbersome.

When you finally push through the tough part and have a new routine, a new perspective, and a new crossroad, new opportunities that are a direct result of a different way of viewing the world and your role in it blossom. When you look at where you are now and how you got there, what decisions did you make? Who did you align yourself with? What relationships are keeping you there?

Complacency satisfies alignment for a moment and plants temporary roots of an understanding of "how a person is" that seems permanent, though that never turns out to be the case. Identities are fluid; yours, mine, and everyone else's. The point of experiencing the modern human condition is to "grow" and cultivate a deeper understanding within the self-actualization realms of Maslow's Hierarchy of Needs, which equates to identity shifts. We should be continuously exploring ourselves to find what we align with that will continuously facilitate our development for optimal capacity.

Does this mean that *all* parts of our identity are constantly changing? Of course, not. The facets that make up the unexplored areas of our identity are only as good as the base they were built upon, hence having a sound understanding and embodiment of who we actually are and are destined to be is critically important.

Identity and History

Beginning with St. Augustine's autobiography, "Confessions," understanding the duality of man and our consistent quests for "self-discovery," "self-description," and "self-assessment" have been challenged by social norms, religion, and globalization. St. Augustine's text was the first written account of identity transformation (a conscious decision to change one's lifestyle from pagan to Christian) which included detailed reflection of personal flaws, mistakes, and events that portrayed him as unheroic and imperfect (Lindholm 2007).

This was remarkably different from the historical literature accounts on identity from Roman and Greek authors which were heavily embedded with great deeds achieved and honorary accolades that praised the individuals being described. Augustine's descriptive accounts regarding his flaws and the responsibility he had to himself (as opposed to his ancestors and family) opened the gateway for expanding personal agency (the ability to direct actions toward a goal) and was not inextricably linked to one's bloodline when understanding the elements of one's identity. This understanding of one's place in the world was described by Plato and later buttressed by

Machiavelli in his classic work, "The Prince," describing oneself and others not as what we wish to be or what we ought to be, but rather as we really are (Lindholm 2007).

This has value and serves as a gateway for honest discourse regarding possibilities and the potential for understanding challenges and the essence of what it means to be a human being. This is a realistic perspective and provides uncontested strength as it is embedded in what is actual and not what is falsely imagined (due to pop culture influences). It provides important insight into the value that we as humans give to the thoughts and words of those within our social groups.

The validation process of seeing ourselves as formed from the opinion of others is heavily influenced by what the famous Genevan philosopher, Jean Jacques Rousseau, called "amour propre," where the thoughts of others regarding ourselves provides self-worth, self-love, and status amongst our peers and increases or decreases our social standing (Dent & Hagan 1998). When you arrive at a level of introspection that allows you to clearly see how others identify where you align in their lives, you begin to see the value in independent and introspective detachment of those same individuals.

Arthur Schopenhauer (a well-known German philosopher) aligned himself with the Buddhist teachings of social detachment and called for the journey within the human condition to be rooted in the release of social expectations and labels of identity to one that is based on self-assessment and value assignment through recognized changes, gains, losses, and enlightenment that is completely introspective (Lindholm 2007). Undoubtedly, there is contention between "amour propre" and "social detachment," yet there is complimentary value in maintaining both as simultaneous possibilities when understanding identity construction and consistent adaptations and formations throughout the course of one's life.

A symbolic example of this is seen in Sri Lanka with the in-depth work done by Gananath Obeyesekere (anthropologist) in Katargama. His 1981 analysis of Hindu-Buddhist priestesses who grew matted hair as a means of fortifying their pact with one of many Hindu gods combined social and personal assessments that meant a lot to individual identity. The symbolic experience of priestesses being "given" matted hair by the gods contributed to a conscious shift of what Gananath termed as objectification or "the expression of private emotions in a public idiom" of their cultural experience within their religious devotion.

As much as the matted hair symbolized an active social and religious relationship, it also served as a coveted self-accomplishment and triumph for the priestesses who had them. The root of their understanding of what the matted locks symbolize came from the value system acquired in a social domain, yet the embodied experience and moments in solitary meditation which cultivated the relationship with the given deity provided the individual prominence to maintain the matted hair.

This model is powerful. Assessing cultural symbols, their subsequent embodiment and production of self-motivation is a recipe that lends itself to identifying the importance of fusing yourself with others as you not only align with them individually, but also socially. Buttressing this notion of cultural and personal symbols and their value in addressing identity is the importance of recognizing the role that imagination of the "other" has. In Max Weber's classic 1905 work, "The Protestant Ethic and The Spirit of Capitalism", the sociological concept of *verstehen* (putting yourself in the shoes of others to see things from their perspective) is elaborated upon as a key ingredient for understanding "the other" and our necessity to embody differing perspectives so that we may understand ourselves better.

This imaginative form of "putting ourselves in another's shoes" is a necessary element in understanding our own identity and how our social interactions are defined through the understanding of others' interpretations. The value that is put on the thoughts and words of those within our social groups as well those outside them contributes to a process of interpreting multiple stimuli on a physical, emotional, and spiritual level. Imagination and role perception adds to our identity and pushes us to consciously seek the *emic* (insider's perspective) while maintaining an *etic* (outsider's perspective) subconscious.

Another cross-cultural example can be found in research done by well-known playwright, Dorinne Kondo, and her 1990 ethnographic (cultural study) text, "Crafting Selves." She elaborates the need to stay away from fostering an identity embedded with selfishness and to focus on crafting a lens of interaction that is based upon sincerity and being attuned to others and their needs, hence encouraging a dependence on others and a reinforcement on relationship alignment. She accounts for this perspective from the time she spent working in a Japanese industrial factory where self-identity was often blurred with social identity and family-corporate relationships.

Her interactions shine light on the confusion fostered between social norms, economics, and industrialized society where moments of social oppression can hinder our ability to be in touch with our own selves or the identity of others. According to Kondo's reflections, it is always possible to retrieve a deeper understanding of "the other" through introspection. Her idea of putting herself in the "other's shoes" results from socializing with factory workers at a remote ethics retreat. It was an experience somewhat comparable to a Western corporate retreat but different in that it combines Japanese forms of spiritual/physical purification, exercise, meditation, cleaning, and shouting (as a means of decompressing and releasing stress).

The idea behind this sort of institution is to suspend the effects of mainstream society where social status, corporate hierarchy, and the "everyday self" often become numb to the intricacies of the human experience and typically put individuals in alignment with one another for who they are in that moment, rather than who society constructs them to be. In other words, it's better to remove labels, titles, and pressures felt from social demands and return to a holistic sense of self that is honest, naked, and authentic with who you actually are and not who society tells you to be.

Aligning Mental Models

In Dr. Peter Senge's groundbreaking 1990 text, "The Fifth Discipline", an invaluable nugget within the decision-making process is highlighted: the role of mental models. His insights are echoed by Dr. Bill Anton in his well-renowned 2015 text, "Ascend: Forging A Path To Your Truer Self". Both experts stress the importance of understanding how mental models are formed, as they are as much cultural as they are biological.

According to Dr. Senge, mental models are deeply held internal images that limit us to familiar ways of thinking and acting. They are comprised of assumptions, previous experiences, images, smells, beliefs, values, ideas, concepts, language, and meaning making. Very often, we are not consciously aware of our mental models or the effect they have on our behavior.

The thing about mental models is that they are associated with lived experiences that have left an impression within the brain's neurocircuitry throughout the course of your life. That impression is tied to biological responses (think neurohormones released when you are happy, sad, scared, etc.) associated with the experience. After reinforced exposure to the same types of experiences or learning, the brain creates neuropathways that become your neurological default and make up a particular mental model. The challenge is that many of us stick to the same mental models throughout life as well as the types of people who were present during their formation. We do not open ourselves to shifting our established circuitry and our subsequent perceptions, as this requires change which is hard.

The many lenses of the life cycle call us to collectively blend our previously lived experiences to figure out what works, what doesn't, who we choose to be around and why they makes sense (or not), as well as better ways to handle circumstances and stressors. For example, how many times have you told someone that you did something because, "That's just how I am and there's no changing me." Is that entirely accurate? Absolutely not. It's who you are consistently choosing to be because it's comfortable, and it's comfortable because that's what you know. Exploring the wilderness of new possibilities presents unknowns that can be ambiguous and scary (Anton 2015). This is a detrimental byproduct of increased luxury afforded to us throughout species progression that often goes unaddressed.

Let's look back at Maslow's Hierarchy of Needs and dissect what our ancestors Australopithecus, Homo Habilis, Homo Erectus, and Homo Neanderthalensis focused upon. Throughout the millions of years of their respective life cycles, they worked through the fundamental pillars of Maslow's hierarchy (physiological, safety, love and belonging) which afforded us (Homo sapiens) the ability to focus on the last two pillars of the pyramid (esteem and self-actualization). This has contributed to our species development, but it has also worked against us as we now find points of contention in almost everything between and amongst different groups.

The conversations we have within social settings (as well as within ourselves) typically relate to differences in beliefs, values, and cultural practices. They have nothing to do with how we are going to migrate from one geographic location to the next for survival, how we are going to endure the upcoming winter, who is going to go with the hunting party to hunt animals to provide food security, etc. Our mental efforts are elsewhere and the biological responses that once kept us alive are now having to morph and accommodate the luxuries afforded to us through our own species development.

We are contending with genetic coding and biological systems that are millions of years old and our modern-day "actualization" has progressed faster than the process of biological evolution which should not be confused with adaptation.

As a species, what we are dealing with now is a superhighway of global information that is not bound or solidified in concrete beliefs or lived experiences; rather, it's built on a façade of identity politics where each individual has their own unique experiences and life stories that take on different shapes throughout the life cycle and affect decisions made at any given time. It is our duty to take ownership of how our decision-making process shifts from one stage of the life cycle to the next and what external factors influence the deductive reasoning process within ourselves as well as others.

Consider the current political feuds that exist at a global level and the impact they have on our financial systems. Politics and finances go hand in hand as they are tied to a projected idea of survival that is rooted in personal beliefs. Consider the act of war. It's well-known that wars typically mean inflation, reduced GDP, and a rise in national debt. How about the cost of presidential elections within a nation that is becoming divided over politicians who proclaim to share beliefs and end up pitting fellow citizens against one another?

This is an example of how groups of people get caught up in the same mental models without attaining a sufficient level of objectivity to ask themselves why. Why are they choosing to believe their respective political parties? Why are they constantly fighting (as opposed to productively debating) with others who have a different opinion? What subconscious cues are being triggered that repeat the same thought processes throughout our neuropathways without them ever being challenged?

Achieving healthy alignment requires you to unpack the silent influences that shift your perceptions and beliefs, particularly when you don't recognize the level of control they have over your daily thoughts and decisions. *Choice is powerful, and not understanding what influences how you make choices is like driving a car with a blindfold and turning the wheel, accelerating, and braking because "it just feels right."*

Aligning With Others

As a species, we are built for survival. We are built to withstand adversity and we are built to be social creatures. This demands an understanding of what it means to align ourselves with others for productive outcomes. We all need to define what "productive outcomes" in relationships look like. Is it a relationship that we're vested in because we can get something that solely benefits us, or is it because we recognize and appreciate there are benefits to both yourself and the other person? This is the tough part of "alignment discipline," being able to discern whether your commitment to a relationship is for your own personal advancement/comfort or for mutual benefit with productive outcomes for everyone involved.

Western society has shaped and molded an acceptance of narcissistic and self-centered behaviors where things are all about the individual. The widespread use of social media platforms has created censored forums that have shaped a vision of reality and belief that encourage folks to do what they want to do, when they want to do it, with whomever they want to do it. This seems reasonable on the surface.

Individuals harnessing their own agency to create a life or pursue relationships of their own choosing makes sense but it falls short of reality.

This era of human existence has forgotten the truth that our species is designed to thrive in community and in harmony with one another. There is no way we would have made it this far had it been thousands of years of "The Me Show." Since we began popularizing social platforms that shun us from having meaningful conversations with neighbors and colleagues or forming new friendships, we have forgotten the value of authentic relationships and community. These platforms encourage misalignment through controlled narratives that we allow to shape what relationships should look like and our place within them.

The contention I have is not with the actual platform itself, it's that the way these platforms are managed and prioritized by pop culture have established them as staples in how we navigate our relationships to others and different social climates. Our ability to stay tuned in to a conversation or focus on a task is slowly dwindling, not because of biological evolution but because of choice.

The more time tasks require, the more we choose not to remain engaged. We are choosing to not give ourselves the time needed to fully understand the concepts we seek to master, believing that a spoonful of partial knowledge is better than a robust gallon. We are choosing to devalue reason, common sense, and the core principles that should bind us together as a culture. We are becoming more consumed with easily obtained simple information and allowing the influx of nonstop data to define our existence and inform us as to what should make sense.

As a species, we have always sought answers. We have explored unknowns and we have banded together to create a more promising and efficient future for generations to come by allowing the brightness that is humanity to truly shine. *What we are experiencing now is a reversal, a reversal in community and what is actually sustainable in keeping us together.* When was the last time you defined principles that align together and contribute to the version of yourself you strive to be? My bet is that you've never done it; and if you've attempted it, you haven't revisited it in quite some time. Yet, you make decisions every single day based on what you believe aligns together to create a normal and healthy perspective of the world, and that's scary.

It's scary to think that the majority of us get up in the morning and begin making decisions because of perceived priorities that have been dictated to us by silent influences rather than our own genuine alignment.

Aligning our beliefs in who we are and what we stand for requires a deep understanding of ourselves that society's current tempo doesn't deem a priority. Rather, the influence of mass marketing and media outlets instruct us on what our priorities should be as well as how others will judge us, not realizing they are victims of the same façade.

The simple truth is that achieving alignment is hard. You need to dig to the inner depths of yourself and bring forth the genuine factors that make you thrive and give you peace. Cutting out exterior influences and returning to your source will push you to find immense discipline as well as freedom in who you are and the value you bring to others in relationships.

But, most of us are not willing to dig deep. We are content with surface-level interactions and simply making relationships transactional since they serve a particular purpose at a given time in our lives and provide an understanding of life that we deem "good enough." This is not how or why we were designed.

The human qualities of compassion, empathy, kindness, love, and the need to feel valued and wanted were not forged within us through transactional relationships. They were formed over millennia of depending on one another, recognizing mutual beliefs that bring us together within a shared identity as opposed to a regularly individualistic one, as well as appreciating the value and privilege of having healthy relationships with others. Somewhere along the line, the valuable concept of "social capital" became tangibly interchangeable with commerce and items for trade.

Author Lyda Hanifan referred to social capital as "those tangible assets [that] count for most in the daily lives of people:

namely goodwill, fellowship, sympathy, and social intercourse among the individuals and families who make up a social unit."

As the Greek storyteller Aesop told us, "You are who you keep." Those directly in your sphere of influence and the people you spend time with are a direct reflection of your values, beliefs, and representations of what the world looks like through your eyes. Knowing the level of influence that others have on you and that you have on others, why would any of us invest in a relationship for strictly transactional purposes? It undermines the entirety of the gift that it is to be human. It reduces our existence down to nothing more than a service contract to "elevate" what we have or the perceived opportunities ahead of us. It also contributes to a degradation of the value we bring to others.

Since the industrial revolution, we have been conditioned to compartmentalize various facets of our lives, including relationships. Think of the work life and personal life separation, individuals claiming that they have a "work wife" or a "work husband" as well as having one standard for acceptable behavior at home and another for acceptable behavior in the workplace. It pressures us to create two separate identities, which we do not do well. Now amplify that. Think of who you portray yourself to be on social media, the conformity you might display with others to avoid "rocking the boat" in discussions or conversations that force you not to be genuine about who you truly are. These are all things that happen continuously and create identity crises for each of us.

If our identities are constantly shifting, then how do we know what we truly stand for? What you stand for is a constant, and every time you shift or tilt the balance of that constant you shake a small piece of your identity. The good news is that you can get it back. You just need to be true to yourself and know what and who you are aligned with and keep those relationships close.

If you want more meaningful and fruitful relationships in your life, be authentic and genuine in your dealings with others. This means allowing yourself to be vulnerable, as there is no façade shielding the essence of who you are, and it opens you up to greater understanding from others. Yes, you run the risk of others throwing that authenticity back in your face, but it allows you to see fear and misunderstanding much faster and forces you to recognize how they are not aligned to having a relationship with you.

The relationships that you belong in make themselves known as those people share your same level of authenticity or at least close to it. They recognize your vulnerability and want to be around it as it represents truth of character, truth of identity, and an incomparable level of confidence as you will have a belief in and an understanding of yourself that most will never give themselves the opportunity to attain, though they would like to.

Strip back the layers on all the relationships you believe you're currently aligned with and ask yourself why. Why are you investing the one thing you can never get back in this life (time) into those people? How are they fortifying the true you? What are the guiding principles that make you better every day that they support and help you grow? If you find it challenging to answer these questions, then you have some inventory items to work on in your life and how it is you are positioning yourself in your relationships with others.

Stop and Think

Allow me to commend you for investing in this book and making your way to this point. Chances are, you've either read books like this before or you've attended at least one conference on how to improve yourself, your life or your relationships. Yet, you've gravitated towards this book, and I'll tell you why... you know that there is something missing. There are things within that are pulling you in directions you may not understand or can feel need to change.

Knowledge, without action, is fruitless. For example, everyone knows how to lose weight but only those who consistently put into action what they know will get the results they desire. Along those lines, what you know about yourself and how often you put it into practice will determine the depths of success you will experience as a fulfilled human being as well as the quality of joy and growth you can experience with others.

Ask yourself:
What is my purpose?
Have I gone all in with the relationship I have with myself?

Have I faced my demons and confronted the darkness they hide in?
Have I settled for a life that is not my truth?
Have I forged the best version of me?
What is the purpose of those I choose to have relationships with?
Do I surround myself with others who support a version of me that is not authentic?

In terms of living a better life, with better relationships, more joy, laughter, success, peace, and love… what are you going to do with the knowledge you've already gleaned from this book? Don't just keep reading, take a moment and answer the questions you just read with brutal honesty.

If you're sick and tired of being sick and tired of not having the relationships and quality of life you desire and deserve, I can't wait for you to turn the page. Up until now, everything we've explored has laid the foundation for what I really want to share in the next chapter so you might want to bring a highlighter!

If you can commit to yourself to put forth the effort it takes to have the right relationship with yourself so you can have the absolute best relationships with others, I can't wait for you to turn the page.

Layer Four:

Listen

Everything You Listen to Influences You

Consider that all the things that pass through your ears and become deciphered through personal filters symbolize what you know—and more importantly, what you don't know. *We don't always choose what we hear, but we always choose what we listen to.*

How others articulate and present information provides an immense amount of data about their emotional temperance, experience, comfort, self-understanding, and confidence. Most of us feel like we have a good pulse on reading people and sizing them up in a first impression, only to be gravely disappointed when our hypothesis on the individual proves to be false. It takes a lot of skill and understanding to know when someone's words and stated intentions are authentic. This reflects how well we're able to decipher what is authentic within ourselves—and what isn't.

As human beings, we are uniquely equipped to make sense and connect context clues to things that may not be directly in front of us. Our brain's neocortex has advanced our ability to imagine outcomes before they become a reality which allows us to think of things and people in different ways that may or may not be accurate. As much as having this imaginative quality has helped us in various social and personal circumstances, it also contributes to our skewed view of what is genuine and authentic.

Gauging our ability to listen means having a clear understanding of all sides of ourselves that are constantly seeking to influence us. Think of the common visual of having a devil on one shoulder and the angel on the other; for most, these little voices are constantly at war.

One will motivate you to get up at 5 a.m. to exercise, while the other will tell you at 4:59 a.m. that you can do it later. One will tell you to eat the extra chocolate chip cookie while the other one will yell "put the cookie down!" knowing that excessive indulgence will only make you feel worse in an hour or two. One will tell you that the person you're talking to seems like a really nice individual because they use words or linguistic patterns that are familiar to you, while the other will tell you all the things you can get out of them, and so on. The point is that no matter the circumstance, your mind is constantly making judgment calls through different filters that are often at odds with each other.

The constant back and forth in your mind is stressful because the authentic you is not aligned. The blessing of our brain being a highly complex organ is that it allows us to work through complicated emotions, thoughts, and experiences. The curse of our brain being a highly complex organ is that it can overcomplicate issues and manipulate us into making hasty decisions and judgements that are often due to misalignment among the facets that make up our identity.

Let's consider the popular paradigm of the body, mind, and spirit trifecta. This line of belief suggests that your body is one entity with its own needs and wants, as are your mind and your spirit. For purposes of context, the spirit represents the internal identity we all carry that harnesses our true, unfiltered self and is connected to others as well as to the source we all come from. Between the body, the mind, and the spirit, how do you know which one to listen to at any given time? Each one presents its own challenges. Your body needs tangible food and drink to sustain itself, your mind needs new stimulation and socialization to maintain homeostasis, and your spirit needs introspective reflection and peace to grow, so how do you achieve equilibrium between all three?

This has been a constant discipline of study within all major religions of the world; monks, priests, pastors, gurus, and the like dedicate themselves to understanding how these three interplay with one another and how to properly balance them as they all feed the identity that is our lived experience on this earth. Any one of these is a lot to try to understand. Of the three, the body has become the easiest to morph and manipulate as we can track and study biological changes that express themselves in what we and others see within our bodies. This is why we have so many institutions dedicated to health, fitness, wellness, etc. The formula is relatively simple to achieve body balance and optimal performance.

Contrarily, the mind and the spirit offer a different level of complexity that is hard to measure and quantify. The fields of sociology, psychology, and anthropology have created measurement tools to assess one's collective consciousness, mental output, brain activity, and sense of purpose. The challenge with these assessments is that they're highly subjective and only provide a snapshot of an individual's prowess on the day the assessment is taken. Things like emotional turmoil, disappointment, excitement, deprivation, etc., can all contribute to inaccurate assessments.

Additionally, there is an incredible bias that presents itself within each of these two domains. As far as balancing between the mental and spiritual, since there is no quantitative biological measurement, it's almost impossible for a third party to evaluate where another individual stands. This is exactly why self-measurement, discipline, and understanding of oneself is paramount. Only you can discern the barriers and blockades that are keeping you from reaching your full potential, and only you can decide which facets of your identity influence you the most.

There is an old native Cherokee story that accounts for two wolves at odds with each other. Each wolf represents a perspective within a young boy who feels conflicted about decisions he needs to make. Upon asking his grandfather which wolf will win the dispute, the grandfather subtly replies, "Grandson, the one you feed the most is the one that will win."

This is impactful and powerful, particularly in the context of understanding which facet of your identity you should listen to as you are making decisions and interacting with others. In a day and age where we put maximum emphasis on the body and physical experiences, we have conditioned ourselves to not expand upon our own mental and spiritual growth.

Most of our interactions have become transactional. Think of what you do when you get hungry; you eat. It's a very simple exchange. Your body shows signs of hunger, so you execute the action of giving it what it needs. How do you achieve this with your mind and spirit? *We have become so focused on immediate satisfaction that we've forgotten the value of providing long-term nutrients to the parts of our being that we cannot see.* We deprive ourselves of spiritual and mental health and don't even know it. Think of how that affects how well you truly know all of yourself and how well you can interact authentically with others.

Most of us are starving for mental and spiritual interactions with each other. We yearn to connect at a much deeper level, but are never taught how to balance the trifecta of identities that comprise our totality. We constantly rely on the tangible transactions that we are accustomed to within the physical world because that's the one that presents the most stimuli and is fed the most. As a society, this has cost us immensely.

Consider the amount of mental illness cases on the rise, the number of broken families, drug dependency, confused and conflicted adolescents and adults, stress and anxiety issues, as well as people simply not knowing their place in the world. This is due to the deprivation of spiritual and emotional needs which creates a disjointed identity and challenges our perception of our place in the world as well as our interpretation of what we're put on this earth to do.

Considering the complexity of the identity trifecta, we are presented with another challenge. How do you know when someone you share a relationship with is being authentic in their communication and intentions? How can we even begin to discern where they fall in the spectrum of being aligned and attuned to their own truth and intentions? The reality is that you can't. There is no possible way for you to make a judgement call like that. The only thing you can do is ensure that your alignment is optimal so you can recognize a misalignment in those you share relationships with. This is the adventure of knowing what to listen to, and when, within yourself, as well as others.

I remember as a twelve-year-old boy meeting a young man named Bob who purchased land from my parents to build his home. He was a tall and very athletic individual who carried himself with poise, class, and a no-BS kind of attitude. Seven months after our first meeting, he became my next-door neighbor and subsequently my boxing and martial arts instructor. He was a former professional fighter with a unique and eclectic background. When I first approached him to learn how to fight, he succinctly and directly told me, "Hurting people and destroying things is easy. Helping people and creating beautiful things takes a lot more work and discipline, so you'll start there." True to form, we did. He gave me a reading list (all the classics) and his bonsai garden behind his house to take care of for twelve straight months. Learning how to physically fight wasn't even an option. Little did I know that he was teaching me how to fight mentally and spiritually, forging the discipline to put aside what I thought I wanted and empowering me with what I needed: the requisite mental fortitude and patience to care for something other than myself, and expanding my mind and understanding of others through literary classics that captured the human essence in its rawest forms.

These were the gems that opened my eyes to the beginning of understanding balance and feeding the internal wolves. After a dedicated year, he began teaching me the sweet science of boxing, as well as Muay Thai kickboxing and Wing Chun kung fu; all the while requiring me to listen to audio books of Shakespeare, Longfellow, and Schopenhauer while training me, truly a challenge when you're a teenager and want to listen to the latest pop and rap songs during a workout. Each training session would be followed by a thirty-minute meditation session and a conversation that had nothing to do with the combative arts, but rather what I learned about myself and the understanding that was being fostered between my mind, body, and spirit. Twenty-three years later, I'm still a student of his.

The most valuable lessons I learned from him had nothing to do with fighting. The lessons that truly made a difference in my life were the ones that instructed me on how to nurture and cultivate the identity trifecta within. Instead of just feeding the body alone, feed the mind and spirit at the same time. To this day, I continuously nourish all three because the moment I stop I can feel the beginnings of misalignment. This affects my ability to communicate objectively, navigate emotions with temperance, understand where others are coming from, and achieve fluidity within my listening abilities. I share this with you to give you a peek into how I keep the three aligned. There are many ways one can achieve alignment; you need to identify what speaks to your value system that should be expressed and lived within the trifecta that makes up your identity.

Your Brain Listening to Others

Your brain is magnificent. There is so much we know about it, and even more that we don't. When you engage in the process of listening, your auditory cortex activates and sifts through sounds, tones, and patterns to make sense of what is being heard. This is all done through synapses, neurons, and neuropathways that have been conditioned over the course of your life to reduce ambiguity around you within your environment. Your brain translates the processed noises into symbols that have meaning and allows you to assign value to them and respond to them (or not).

Many factors come into play when considering how your brain makes sense of what and who you're listening to. In relationships, you must consider the following variables:

1. How do you value the person you're conversing with?
2. What does the conversation mean to you?
3. How does the conversation benefit others you may be aligned with?
4. Where do you want the relationship to go?

These questions matter because your time matters; your time matters because your existence is comprised of only so many hours and so many days to make the most of. In exchanges between human beings, every word, impression, and reaction is measured, symbolized, and kept in our memory bank. Recall what I mentioned earlier about your brain creating shortcuts to make sense of the world so that it doesn't expend unnecessary energy. This is no different.

In relationships, your brain approaches every conversation with preconceived notions of who you are talking to, what they mean in your life, what you mean in theirs, and the future of the relationship (all elements of *framing*, as previously described). This level of data processing is more often than not watered down because our preconceived notions are often out of alignment with the person we share the relationship with.

For example, if I were to approach a conversation with my wife with an assumption about what her responses will be, I will have set an expectation that I'll be measuring and judging her responses as to whether my expectations were met or not. That is the tough part of how our brains listen. In the quest for efficiency, there are important details missed that require a new perception and deeper understanding of the relationship itself. Challenging this model means confronting our own understanding of life and the people we choose to have in it; the brain does not like this. It's hard, cumbersome, and can be neurologically and emotionally taxing, but is very necessary.

Understanding your brain means comprehending and embodying how your mental processes work as well as the influence they have on your interpretation of those around you. Data has been extracted from every relationship you've ever had, and your brain has used this data to contour what interactions should look like. Quite often, this framing doesn't allow for an involuntary way to view others differently, let alone yourself. That's why it's crucial to understand how your brain is listening so you can begin the quest of comprehending how others listen to what you're communicating. Recognizing the filters that make up your decisions and judgment processes calls for challenging questions regarding your listening abilities.

What do you choose to listen to? What portions of your brain are being constantly stimulated, challenged, and forced to grow? What portions of your brain are stagnant or neglected? This brings us back to the identity trifecta of body, mind, and spirit, and your ability to feed the deficient areas to achieve equilibrium among the three. Your brain is no different. Knowing what portions of it you are feeding creates a level of awareness to understand where imbalances exist to attain progressive growth. For example, if you are constantly listening to music that has violent lyrics, screaming and the like, you're feeding areas of your brain that will eventually create neuropathways geared for a consistent dose of violent/aggressive thoughts and emotions.

Conversely, if you balance your exposure to such thought patterns with audiobooks, classical music, or music in languages that are new to you, you will create new neuropathways as well as different perspectives on what your "normal" thought patterns should be.

Balancing neurohormonal regulation is not easy, particularly in a time where there is an abundance of information flowing through platforms we rely on. Think of all the social media sites that produce "fake news" and conjure emotions of fear, doubt, and insecurity in the stability of our country as well as our fellow citizens. It's rampant. Yet, some of us stay glued to these outlets, and though we may say that we know better, the recommendations and stories presented sway our subconscious mind and trigger our imaginations as to what "could be" even if we don't consciously dwell on it.

Your brain is funny like that. It will hold onto austere thoughts and recommendations, and after repeated exposure, will start finding their fabricated connections to your reality. Over time, you may convince yourself they're real simply because that's what you have been consistently feeding your brain, rather than challenging yourself to create a new lens through which to view the world or the information you're receiving. This is why understanding how your brain deciphers information is important.

The processing of information that you selectively listen to is what's maintaining, stagnating, or growing the understanding of your potential and the potential of others you share relationships with. Your brain will always find ways to connect thoughts, emotions, patterns, and behaviors. That's what it's designed to do. From the music you listen to, videos you watch, and the conversations you participate in, the real-time data that's being transmitted to you through your ears has a profound impact on the depth and quality of your listening skills within the relationships you invest in.

How to Listen to Others

So, how do you determine the quality of listener you are? Is it reflected in your comprehension of what's being said, or is it measured by how the person you're conversing with feels about you and the time you're sharing? We all have conversations where we appear to be engaging with someone but are not actively listening in detail to what they're saying. Think of the "Yes, dear" type of response, as well as the "I hear you," or "I get it" clichéd rebuttals.

These are affirmatory statements that may make someone feel that you're aligning yourself with what they're sharing, but in reality, you're waiting for them to say something that resonates with you as true engagement.

Being fully engaged requires you to be completely present in conversation. It requires you to suspend preconceived notions and assumptions about where the person is taking the conversation and allow them to go where they feel it should without you feeling disappointed. This means controlling your facial expressions, the internal energy you may be harnessing because of what they're saying and having the discipline to not allow your emotions to overcome the logic necessary to have a fruitful discussion. *Conversation is not a race to completion; it's a journey that you have to be willing to go on with the other person.*

Japanese culture preaches a concept called *Mushin* which literally translates to "no mind." It was a popular sentiment back in the time of the samurai, as it would push the combatants to relinquish all internal distractions to be completely focused on the fight at hand. It is the pinnacle of targeted thought suspension and allows us to be completely present, in-tune, and in the moment of whatever activity we're dedicating our time to. For those you share relationships with, this is the quality of interaction, listening, and engagement you should bring to the table.

Engaged listening means being specifically tuned into a conversation and offering original thoughts, emotions, and mindful suggestions to further the discussion with the person/people you are speaking with.

Most people are limited in how well they can articulate themselves. Not finding the right words to convey a thought, they become overwhelmed with emotion when recalling life experiences, experience fear and nervousness over how others will respond, and have difficulty choosing what and what not to say. Not understanding themselves or their lived experiences in a clear and concise manner can contribute to communication and listening challenges. Your job as someone "in the know" is to create a platform for dialogue that does not contribute to further complications. How do you this? There are six simple steps:

1. **Meet their energy at the beginning of the conversation.**
   a. When you match someone's energy/body language, they find commonality and middle ground, which equates to comfort. This opens the gateway for mutual dialogue. It doesn't mean that you keep your energy at the same level throughout the duration of the conversation. You merely begin the conversation this way.

2. **Ask more than you tell.**
   a. Ask questions that pertain to topics the person you are conversing with is focused on. This is important. You need to show genuine engaged interest in what the individual is sharing. Their perception of you and the quality of interest you have in them depends upon it.

3. **Ask their opinion on things that matter to you.**
   a. People want their thoughts to be heard. They want to know that you're not just listening, but that you genuinely value what it is that they have to say about things that interest you. When they feel their thoughts are valued, they will view dialogue as a mutual exchange based on mutual interest and respect.

4. **Share direct thoughts that are based upon their opinion.**
    a. Take their thoughts into consideration and value them, but ultimately you should not judge them or change your perspective of them because of a difference in opinion. Take their thoughts and find points of intersection with things you want to share. Combining their opinion with what you want to converse about will create an active environment of "thought blending" that encourages greater connectivity.

5. **Share your thoughts and wait for their reactions.**
    a. Ideally, you want them to reciprocate the exact level of engagement you display. Most will not know how to do that, so it may take time to create a mutual runway for symbiotic dialogue.

6. **End the conversation with the next one in mind.**
    a. Referring to future interactions between you and someone else expresses your commitment to remain engaged with the person you're in a conversation with. Simply parting ways by saying, "Talk to you later" with no mention of what "later" means is ambiguous, and your brain does not like ambiguity (and neither does theirs).

Listening to Measure Commitment

When done correctly, the art of listening will typically tell you more about a person than they can voluntarily tell you about themselves. When you know what to listen for and look for, their ethos and truth will shine through. This requires an ability to separate what we *think*, which is full of assumptions and biases, from what is actually being expressed and communicated by the other person. When we're trying to figure out whether a relationship is worth committing to or not, this matters.

Commitment is a pivotal facet in any life endeavor. Nothing is easy, and everything requires some level of sacrifice and patience. When swimming in the pool that is relationship management and growth, your willingness to commit to knowing someone else and allowing a relationship to work requires an understanding of the other person that isn't seasoned with biases and assumptions; you should strive to be a blank canvas within your initial interactions. This doesn't mean that you're not authentic; it means that you've developed the discipline and awareness to know that your own biases and assumptions can sway your judgement and may not allow you to listen with clarity and empathy.

This brings us full circle to knowing how to listen to yourself and the things that motivate thoughts, emotions, and perceptions you hold at any given time. The first step in suspending those thoughts is to release their influence on you, which means you're releasing assumptions that are fed by the data you're receiving from the other person. This allows you to measure the level and depth of commitment that you're willing to have with the other person and decide whether your mind, body, and spirit want to forge an alignment with them.

Take, for example, a conversation you have with a work colleague. The length and depth of commitment you're willing to have in that relationship is vastly different than the depth of commitment you have with your child. The distance you're willing to go to change your own assumptions and biases to fully understand your child is vastly different from how far you're willing to go for someone you're involved with from a business perspective. I'm not suggesting that all relationships should carry the same depths and commitment you have with your children. I'm suggesting that you should be critical and analytical of yourself and the energy it takes to build the right kind of relationship with those in your social circles that will support positive outcomes.

We want to avoid wasting our time with relationships that may do us harm in the long run and recognize our level of commitment to understanding the other person. If the commitment level is low, and that's indicated by your unwillingness to adapt while listening with a clear and empty filter, you may very well be investing time in a relationship that you will not nurture in the long run.

This is also a measure of your emotional temperance and positioning. Different things will motivate us depending on the intentions we have for the relationship. If you're willing to bend and be pseudo-open-minded to make it seem like you're actively listening and sufficiently interested in them to get something out of them, you're compromising your own identity for a superficial outcome. We all do this. We say or act in a manner that the other person is amenable to so we can "get on their good side" so we can get something out of them. This can be very toxic, as our motivation is not rooted in creating an authentic relationship with them. Rather, we simply want something out of them.

Throughout our lives, motivation doesn't just happen. There are strings attached. Strings that speak to your heart and mind, and symbolize facets of who you are and who you want to be. Get to know your motivators and why they mean so much to you. When you have a good grip on what they are and the nature of their influence on your brain, you must question why they exist.

What has happened in your life to make those motivating factors so powerful? What role do they play in deciding who you align yourself with and commit to? Is the initial motivation enough to keep you committed to a relationship that will blossom and mean something more than a transactional interaction? It should, but it should also adapt as the relationship grows into changing circumstances that surround your life, the relationships in it, and the motivation to continue being a part of it.

LAYER FIVE:

Communicate With Next Steps in Mind

Ikigai

We've covered some ground up to this point. Identity, emotions, understanding ourselves, valuing others, and things to consider before committing to a relationship—all necessary in making sense of ourselves so that we can facilitate continuous growth within our relationships. Once we've made the decision to commit to a relationship, how do we keep growth at the tip of the spear in our interactions? How do we live and interact with others to promote a sense of fulfillment and something to always look forward to?

The Japanese have a concept called *Ikigai*. It means "a reason for being," and it complements the concept of self-mastery and its connection to your source and purpose for existence. It combines passion, love, mission, needs, vocation, profession, and a few other critical elements. The Venn diagram on the following page was created to explain how each element of the concept connects.

Each one of these domains contributing towards your life's fulfillment require relationships for validation. Your profession will always be centered on individuals engaging

with you. Your passion, mission, and vocation will depend on others to grow, while figuring out what you are good at will require feedback from other people to gauge just how "good" you really are. These domains call for varying perspectives, insights, and exchanges and the quality of your interactions with others will determine what they mean to you and your life.

Every single one of us make a choice each day: we choose to either see the world in the same consistent light that contributes to the vision we've constructed and our interpretation of how it works, or we choose to challenge and change our perspective based on how our view of ourselves and others has shifted.

When you "go through the motions" in your relationships, you are doing exactly that; you're choosing to see the world and the people in it that same way on a regular basis. It's predictable, and your brain likes that. But is it real? Is that the objective truth? The answer for most of us is no, it's not.

It's simply a stage of different characters we direct within our minds to facilitate the show that we perceive our lives to be, and we want to keep the turbulence as low as possible. This presents challenges because we're not leading ourselves to grow as individuals, and we're certainly not facilitating an environment that allows others to push us toward a better version of ourselves. This is understandable, as it can be scary to make changes. It's scary to challenge the current understanding of ourselves as well as push the depth of interaction we have with others. It means that we must be more vulnerable, honest, naked, and rawer than we've ever been to successfully break into new bounds of understanding.

Accomplishing this calls for us to be very smart and strategic with our relationship's "next steps." Do we want to continue to "go through the motions" and keep things "status quo," or do we want to challenge our assumptions (as well as theirs) to expose new parts of ourselves and our respective relationships?

Over time, going through the motions becomes a mundane process, and the mystique as well as curiosity of relating to/ with another person loses its charm. This is dangerous, and lends itself to the formation of tears in the fabric of what that other person means in our lives as well as how we value our time, purpose, and meaning.

Currently, the divorce rate in the United States hovers around 40%–50% for first-time marriages. There are several external factors that contribute to the reason for divorce, but the internal factors that become misaligned among couples is seldom studied or understood. Why? Because it's hard to quantify emotions, deprivations, and feelings of being misunderstood, bored, frustrated, etc. Particularly when they may have started as something small at the beginning of the relationship, went unaddressed, and then snowballed into issues that catastrophically repelled both individuals from one another.

The same applies to business partnerships and relationships. On average, close to 80% of all business partnerships fail. Whether it be from disagreements about money, management, or overall commitment, there are misalignments that become present throughout the course of the relationship. For most, business partnerships make sense at conception as each member can fulfill a need to make the business successful. *The key words here are "make the business successful," not "make you and your partners successful as human beings"* which is where a big problem lies.

Marriages are the same. Most folks commit to a marriage because of how much they love, or think they love, another person, when in reality they love what the other person does for them and how they make them feel about themselves. This is a battle with the selfish parts of ourselves that requires confrontation each of us seldom have.

The bleak and ugly points we often refuse to see are constantly winking at us, and we turn a blind eye and mask them in how "good" or "wonderful" others say we are or what we deserve. This is why layers one through three are so important in establishing relationships on the right foot and maintaining them. Framing your relationships to promote mutual growth and positive next steps to achieve that growth is where the brick and mortar resides in constructing a firm and reliable foundation for every relationship you're in.

Your Next Step Should Always Be An Investment

Why do we water plants? We water plants so they can grow, flourish, contribute to the environment's aesthetic, and of course, they bring us pleasure in their beauty.

Why do we exercise? To ensure that our health is optimal and to maintain our quality of life so we can be our best for others and ourselves.

Why do we walk away from others? To gain a new sense of clarity, peace, and understanding.

When making the decision to invest in any relationship in our lives, identifying what we are hopeful for within the relationship as well as what we want it to mutually mean is vital. This is the nature of a good investment. In a very literal sense, when you look at what you invest your money in, you're doing so in hopes of generating a positive return. No one decides to invest their hard-earned dollars without carefully analyzing the pros and cons, as well as the goals and expectations of what the investment can do for them, not to mention the nature of the investment and its potential impact upon others. In that same vein, no financially sound person keeps their money in an investment that is constantly losing value and causing stress. They liquidate and get out!

If we're that critical about how we make moves and plan next steps with our money, shouldn't we do the same with our relationships? Shouldn't we be exceedingly mindful about our investment of time, emotions, peace, and carefully consider how others will influence our identity?

We seldom look at relationships in this light. We rarely take the time to understand how each shift in a relationship will contribute either to our growth or to our detriment, as well as that of the other person. Is that sound? Is that truly the best way to manage time and energy that can never be replaced? Absolutely not. It's frivolous, careless, and wasteful to ourselves as well as others, yet we do this on a regular basis because we don't view our relationships in the same light as other commodities that we keep near and dear to our hearts. In reality, *your bank of relationships and who you choose to be around will shape and mold your identity in silent ways that will creep up on you and influence your thoughts and behaviors.* This heavily influences your quality of life as well as the version of you the world gets exposed to which contributes to constructed self-validation.

Think of how you've learned everything in your life. Were you born with an innate knowledge of your surroundings?

Did you automatically step into different social situations and know exactly how to act, what to say or how to discern what's appropriate or not, etc.? No, you didn't just know those things at birth. You learned them over time from others, which means that you learned by imitating others. That is the learning process. As social creatures, we learn how to respond, act, and manage our emotions through what we see in others.

Throughout many of their literary works, the great Greek philosophers Aristotle and Plato elaborated on the concept of imitation and the importance of recognizing the innate capacity and gravitation we all have to it. Simply stated, *we all learn through imitation*. Whether it is witnessed directly, heard, or read about, imitation makes up an important facet of how we interact with the world and the people in it.

Think of everything you know how to do. Analyze who you learned it from and how it became indoctrinated into who you are and how you act. We forget where we pick up these traits, characteristics, and skills, as we take pride in being able to do things ourselves, believing that our unique fusion of skillsets makes us special or unique and forgetting that what we know was learned outside of ourselves. As Francis Bacon said, "There is no new thing upon the earth," meaning that we may think that something about ourselves is unique, but there's truly nothing new or unseen in our essence, our interactions, or our being. *This is why making the right investments within the relationships we choose to be in matters so much. You're going to imitate them, and they're going to imitate you.*

Consider that the next time you commit to a relationship with the hope of being able to change somebody or "make them better." Understand that there's a very real opportunity cost if you fail to consider how their influence and impact may sway you to be a version of yourself you may not like. Though it may not feel that way, the symbiotic nature of how we exchange information and experience requires a highway of inter-relatability that demands you pour yourself into someone and they into you.

If you are constantly in a rut with someone and you find it difficult to see how important investing in the next step with them is, go back to the drawing board of why you committed to the relationship. *There should never be stagnation in the investment of your time into others.* The last position you want to be in is doing things that you don't genuinely and authentically believe in, yet you continue to do them because it's the norm that's become established. This is the beginning of stagnation that can have severe consequences for you and those who love you.

Trust is Communication's Currency

There is nothing more valuable in a relationship than trust—trust in yourself and your intentions as well as trust in the other person and their intentions. The difficulty with trust is how fast you can lose it. Simply not following through on something you said (or they said) would get done, or something as silly as being presented with hearsay about one's intentions can cause a massive dynamic shift in how a relationship is managed, as well as how it's perceived.

Earning trust—and more importantly, maintaining trust—demands authenticity. It demands being honest and transparent about who you are and what you want within a relationship. Vice-versa, it requires a mind that's open to other viewpoints rather than reacting to them with harsh judgement at first blush. It requires flexibility in communication, patience, and strategic alignment to ensure that values are equally expressed, and differences are equally respected.

This is a cornerstone when considering what direction to take a relationship. Each touchpoint, interaction, and experience that's shared paints a little more on the canvas that is the body of mutual interactions. As any good artist would tell you, the movements, flow, and palette within a work of art all depend on what comes to mind after the previous brush stroke. Deciding next steps in a relationship is the same. *The quality of the last interaction you shared with the other person will always depict the perceived quality of the next interaction.*

You could have a relationship that's been thirty years in the making, and all it takes is one turbulent experience with the individual expressing themselves in a manner that isn't "normal" to inject a seed of doubt into your heart and mind about who they are the next time you're with them.

We know that our brains are wired to look for danger so that we can stay alive, and that wiring applies to social relationships, as well. Anything outside of the ordinary will trigger a red flag, and you'll start doubting the other person. This is why consistency is so important as it forges our understanding of what is "ordinary." More often than not, gaps in relationship growth are caused by gaps in our interactions with each other. When we go through the motions in relationships without being mindful of how to continuously make the relationship grow, we begin opening gates for uncertainty and unpredictability based off roads the other individual may take that have an influence on who they are, thus challenging our perception of them when a new trait or characteristic is displayed.

Seven Layers of Successful Relationships

For example, how many marriages have ended because a spouse was leading a double life? Sometimes, they were able to keep it up for a year or two, while others were able to maintain it for over a decade. The question everyone inevitably asks is, "How can a human being possibly keep such a double life a secret from someone they've sworn their life to?" All the while, the spouse who was being duped may have had an inclination, or maybe felt something in their dynamic was off, but were in denial. The quality of their communication may have shifted, the depth of their interactions and intimacy may have changed, or the priority and excitement of time spent together wasn't the same as it had been in the beginning.

That is the truth shining through, and their brain, instincts, and wherewithal speaking to them. We were designed to have these inclinations within ourselves. This supports why maintaining authenticity and growth in every interaction we have in our relationships is important. *We need to see others grow, and we need to grow with them.* Anything outside of that lends itself to disruption in the dynamics of the relationship where we convince ourselves that why they act a certain way or respond in a certain way isn't the red flag it appeared to be.

The unique thing about deceit is that it is directly tied to the part of your brain called the amygdala which does a phenomenal job of adapting by developing new ways of presenting and processing information. The key word here is *adapting*. You get to choose how your brain adapts and what it adapts to, which ultimately becomes your established behavior pattern.

This is a large part of the challenge when lies compound and have a snowball effect. Facing the embarrassment and shame associated with coming forward with the truth becomes too overwhelming, and the default is to keep the lies and deceit going; this requires constant adaptation and manipulation of what you know the truth to be.

When dishonesty becomes a go-to, your brain adapts to how the result of the lie made the others person feel as opposed to focusing on the stress one experiences when engaging in dishonest behavior. Getting away with things by simply using a play on words, omitting facts, or shifting how information is presented based on a personal agenda creates a sensation of stress mixed with immediate reward that the brain can become addicted to. This is the effect of neuroplasticity and having an organ that is constantly tweaking itself based on established mental models contrasting with newly interpreted data, emotional balance or imbalance, spiritual wherewithal (or lack of it), as well as an authentic understanding of who you are (and who you're not).

When you choose to be less than completely genuine and honest, your brain expends a *ton* of energy. You must cover the bases of who you're pretending to be while sustaining who you actually are. This is not easy, and it's not what we were designed for, yet we have created a social environment for ourselves where this has become the norm. Think of how social media presents double lives. Folks post things to their personal pages and paint a grandiose image of themselves or in the manner they wish to be perceived, knowing that it isn't real.

They do it for the temporary satisfaction and gratification of presenting "what could be" without coming to terms and accepting what currently is. The more they post the inauthentic version of themselves, the more they begin to believe in the falsehoods they receive praise and validation for. There is a very real biological consequence associated with this as serotonin and dopamine are released in micro-amounts, making people who do this temporarily feel good or accomplished and enjoy the notion that they're living a life that others envy. The sad part is that sustainable happiness is found in confronting and completely understanding their present selves so they can build truth in their relationships.

As an entrepreneur, I've witnessed so many things within my journey that irk me. One of these is the phrase, "Fake it, 'til you make it." Why in the world would we influence young, vibrant, and ambitious minds to fake anything? Why would we contour their framing of business, interactions, relationships, and offerings in anything less than a genuine framing of things being presented exactly the way they are? This is not only true in the entrepreneurial world, it is so rampant in the marketing and sales tactics of major global corporations that's it's become orthodoxy. Deceit and false promises are everywhere.

Our modern society accepts this as normal, then questions why things don't work out the way they expected them to when the delivery is not what they thought it would be. Fake it 'til you make it has become engrained in the very fabric of how we do things as a culture. *This is why honesty, sincerity and trust are the most valuable things you can bring to any relationship. It separates you from what our "normal" has become as a society and fosters the ability to speak to the heart instead of appealing to a temporary fad.*

Each Step Counts

You are constantly being tested and evaluated, just as you are constantly testing and evaluating others. Every interaction is an evaluation of solidarity and consistency, though we often do not recognize it as such. When we think of an evaluation, we think of a formal process that analyzes what is being done with an outcome that is determined to be favorable or not. The type of evaluation I'm referring to is similar, but more subtle; your subconscious combines mental models that form the way you see the world and everyone in it. Each touchpoint you have as well as next steps within an interaction define the essence of the relationship expectations you will have that are evaluated against those established models. This recalls the previous concept of *framing* and what initial thoughts/blueprints are of someone when entering in a relationship.

Your governing standard of measurement will be based on the framing you have of yourself as well as the other person while contributing to how you contour your thoughts when deciding where you want the relationship to go. This is why keeping the next step of a relationship at the forefront of your mind is important.

You want relationships to grow and mutually benefit all parties involved. Anything outside of that is a digression in your own growth and will require time and energy to get back on track. This isn't always a bad thing since some relationships are worth drudging through the mud for in order to get back to the shoreline, while others are not. That is where you need to decide how you want to spend your time and who you want to spend your time with.

You do not want to force a relationship into alignment. Timing, values, principles, culture, patience, and understanding are things that must come from within to generate a genuine connection with someone. This is not to be confused with making a hard choice and doing things you don't want to do out of comfort or conditioning. Rather, this is recognizing that you're working towards committing to relationships with people who relate to your journey and can contribute to the growth of your identity while you contribute to theirs. Using this as a North Star for how you progress forward in relationships will enhance your level of understanding and relatability with others.

Is it possible to make decisions in a relationship that seem to move it in the right direction, but actually move it in the wrong direction? Absolutely. It happens all the time, but why? Why do we mislead ourselves (and others) with decisions about what our role is within a relationship as well as what we interpret as good or bad for the relationship? Is it even about the relationship or could it be that we're mismanaging ourselves? Circle back to the earlier narrative in Chapter One about how we lie to ourselves by fabricating an understanding of things we've committed to without truly understanding or believing in the *why* that propelled us to it. How many relationships have you been part of that became mismanaged, failed, hit a roadblock, etc? What feelings came to the forefront that caused us to abandon what our initial hopes and expectations were in the beginning of the relationship?

It's always easy for us to look at the other person and point the blame at them, failing to recognize that somewhere along the way there was a misalignment between you both that you didn't pay attention to. That bump in the road created a domino effect that influenced both of you to see the relationship in a different light and devalued the time you shared together.

When these sorts of bumps are ignored or tucked under the relationship's rug, there begins to be a hoarding process where small misalignments are pushed to the side and are never re-aligned. This process compounds, eventually breaking the relationship. Sometimes it is amicable, while at other times it can be an absolute mess. If both individuals have taken the time, consideration, and care with each step towards growth in the relationship, then the bumps will be addressed immediately, and micro re-alignments will be made throughout the relationship as opposed to dealing with massive gaps that began as subtle inconsistencies.

If, while addressing small re-alignments along the way, you encounter a significant challenge, then perhaps the initial alignment was not as strong as you thought. There is, then, a very real possibility that you convinced yourself that you were more aligned with the person than you actually were. Far too often, while looking at the person we're in the relationship with, we align ourselves with the relationship's benefits as a tool to achieve those outcomes, when in reality, we never took the appropriate next steps for the health of the relationship and betterment of both people involved. This reinforces why each next step in a relationship should always consider the quality and authenticity of the time being spent with one another.

If there are misalignments between you and the other person, they need to be addressed. The moment you choose not to address them is the moment you begin to put the relationship in neutral thereby opening the possibility of rolling backwards with no brake to stop you.

LAYER SIX:

Stay Open to Possibilities

Who Do You Want to Be?

This layer highlights the relationships you currently have, and more importantly the ones yet to come.

Ask yourself, "Who am I really?" and "Who am I not?" Define them both. Now consider the person you want to be five years from now. Do you see yourself having the exact same relationships with the exact same people? I would suppose that you don't. Of course, you will have core relationships that contribute to your identity and validation as a human within your family, tribe, and professional circles, but there should be growth and maturity. This growth should lead you to want to meet others who are excelling in a similar fashion that you can pour into while they pour into you.

Knowing that our brains are wired for efficiency and figuring things out as soon as it possibly can, what does it take to recognize potential relationships we should be open to that will infuse us with additional purpose, drive, and meaningful impact?

Objectively viewing new possibilities as steps forward in the relationship you have with yourself will have a ripple effect on relationships you share with others, and that's a good thing. This doesn't mean that you don't listen to your gut. On the contrary, this means that you're not only listening to your gut, but you're understanding why and when your gut is telling you something. This is being attuned to your own mental models and challenging them and the role they play in the relationships you choose to invest in as a means of discovering greater meaning for your life.

Relationships should be assets to the currency that is your quality of life, not liabilities that cost you time, energy, and constant disappointment. Although some level of disappointment is bound to happen in any relationship, what we learn and how we re-align ourselves post-disappointment contributes to the outcome and resiliency of all life's relationships.

In neuroscience, we find Hebb's Rule, which states, "Neurons that fire together wire together." Meaning, the more frequently that neuron cells in the brain are activated together, the more they become associated with each other. Think of it this way, when you consider how you become "good" at something, more than likely, you're very efficient at it. If you are efficient at it, your brain has created neurocircuits within its synaptic (nerve) activity to make whatever the task is relatively easy. The same thing happens when we're making sense of relationships and assessing what a relationship is as well as what it could be. The "what it could be" part is where our imagination plays a big role and our ability to regulate our own desires and models becomes prevalent.

Having previously established mental models clash with the possibility of new mental models opens the door to possibilities. Depending on the context of what we're considering, the possibility for a new way of thinking about something can be fantastic or terrifying. In this circumstance, we're focusing on the possibility for new mental models as well as ways of viewing relationships that are more productive to achieving a sound sense of fulfillment in one's life.

For example, many years ago I had a client who came from an incredibly loving and dedicated family. The foundation of his mental models was established by parents who knew the value of staying open to possibilities and living a life centered around discipline, growth, and measured success. The relationships he was able to forge because of his upbringing and extended family were of tremendous value and opened his life to several possibilities of "what could be."

As he entered adulthood, he met a young lady he chose to enter in an intimate relationship with who he later married. Unbeknownst to him, the alignment between them was "off." Some things made sense, while others did not, but he never gave himself the chance to self-discover and unveil the unknown parts he could grow into, let alone the role that he would later have in the relationship. The eventual gaps that began as small cracks became exceedingly clear as time went on, but they were never addressed. She had not accomplished much with her life but looked to him to open the doors of "what could be" for her and he became fixated with her dependence on him. This dependency ended up becoming a "daddy-daughter" complex where she slowly achieved complete emotional dominance over him and what was once the beginnings of his self-understanding became cloaked in the version of himself that she wanted him to be.

The particularly disturbing part about this is the digression he experienced. As a means of living the life she wanted, he sacrificed mental models and habits that were productive in providing him with growth-centric relationships for new models that were completely based on appeasing her insecurities. This led to an identity crisis where he denounced relationships with lifelong friends and family while he morphed himself into a person he later found grave contention with. By closing off the possibilities of "what could be" for his life, he went to an extreme that sacrificed his ability to achieve self-awareness and an authentic understanding of who he truly is.

His sense of validation became based upon satisfying his wife's demands, needs, wants, and wishes instead of a symbiotic and complementary co-existence with each other. He chose to have his identity become an appeasement to a misaligned relationship that led to a full-blown mental breakdown and the loss of his authentic self which is incredibly traumatic. The byproduct has been that his own self-worth and social capital have become severely diminished.

This is the dangerous side of closing off possibilities of *what could be* for yourself and the relationships you're committed to. When someone convinces themselves that they're locked into a relationship that exudes toxicity due to misalignment, they open themselves up to ignoring their truth because they don't want to face failure. *The reality of our truth is that it's found through failure because failure is the first step in recognizing our own misalignment.*

If I'm constantly unhappy, angry, and complaining, it's clear that I failed in my decision-making abilities somewhere along the line. I misaligned myself internally, and in turn, I've misaligned myself externally with others who I've committed to investing in. This has a very real impact on your brain's cognitive understanding of how it is that you can attain new ways of viewing yourself as well as the world.

Your brain's prefrontal cortex is a fascinating and exceedingly important area. It spearheads all complex cognitive functions including imagination and higher-level thinking. When you stop challenging the prefrontal cortex to imagine various possibilities for yourself and your life, stagnation occurs; the understanding you have of yourself and those you choose to relate to in life begins to change. The brain's ability to allow for coding, meaning making, and fulfillment begin to shift and adapt to the stagnation and opens you up to making decisions that are not rooted in sound understandings of authentic happiness and self-fulfillment.

The example above is just one case of millions that have happened throughout the history of human beings that lend itself to recognizing why it's so important to remain open to creative possibilities within relationships—as well as within yourself.

I've worked with people who challenged themselves to achieve awareness of the possibilities that exist for their lives and have blossomed into wholesome, healthy, and robust leaders who know how to recognize deficiencies within their own understandings of relationships and what they need to do for mutual growth in relationships.

Remaining open to new possibilities takes courage. It means that you openly and willingly accept the unknown parts of yourself that will eventually make themselves known as long as you consistently provide an approach to life that encourages exposing them.

Recognition is always the first step; garnering the mental and intestinal fortitude to think about how you will act on it is the second. The third step is executing it and applying the lessons learned to your life. This is crucial as you continue to unveil the parts of yourself that keep you from staying open to change, new horizons, and more fulfilling ways to relate to yourself, as well as others, where authenticity and truth reign.

Knowing When a Relationship Has Been Exhausted

There is a "right time to walk away" from a relationship.

Ideally, recognizing misalignment sooner, rather than later, allows you to govern how much time will be needed to get a relationship back on track or whether the misalignment is too difficult to adjust. The challenge with this is the ping-pong effect we go through that pushes us to stay and (hopefully) work through the issues as opposed to completely adapting to the other person or simply walking away from the relationship. For relationships that are longstanding, it's often more difficult to walk away than for relationships that are new.

As they have contributed to our identity and purpose in the world, relationships that have been in our lives for years have emotional elements that keep us dedicated to the growth of our interactions with the other individual. These relationships develop more complexity, particularly when we begin to grow at a faster pace than those around us. Our ability to see things within ourselves that perpetuated the initial commitment to the other person may change through self-discovery and become increasingly difficult to hold onto as you reach new levels of awareness, humility, and objectivity.

So, how do you know when it's time to walk away? How do you know when a relationship has become detrimental to your growth, purpose, and meaning as a human being? The answer has everything to do with the understanding you have of your personal constitution as well as the parts that contribute to the growth of where and who you want to be.

Many of us have relationships that are "non-negotiables." These are the relationships that, because of the important role they play in defining and validating our existence, will always be in our lives, no matter what. For example, it could be parents, siblings, children, etc. which you cannot deny because of the biological and emotional attachments associated with them. You may be able to put distance within these relationships, but you will never be able to completely walk away from them since they are embedded in your heart and soul, and you have undeniable attachments to these individuals.

That doesn't mean that all of these relationships are healthy and productive, but completely walking away is exceedingly difficult. With other relationships, our frequent evaluation and analysis brings things to light that should be questioned and explored, assuming a mutual commitment to malleability and adaptability. When a person you share a relationship with begins to function in the world of absolutes and it becomes "their way or the highway," you have a red flag. This could be temporary and simply require a discussion to get them to see a different perspective, but it must be addressed immediately. Don't push it off into a corner and ignore it. That's how resentment begins, which leads to additional problems within your relationship dynamic.

Absolutes make sense when it comes to our morals and values and how we govern our individual actions. When on the quest for enhanced connectivity with others, operating in "expected absolutes" becomes dangerous as the true essence and nature of a healthy relationship is to "relate to one another," not to establish one person's will as a defining pillar within the relationship. Relatability is the backbone for achieving social capital and social capital is what drives consensus in what we do and who we should be around.

Well-known medical anthropologist, Bill Dressler, has done immense work and research in the field of *cultural consonance*. This field is dedicated to understanding the role of culture in health outcomes. How well someone blends in and projects the ideals and staples of the culture surrounding them has an influence on mental and physical health outcomes. Think about it. When we begin to measure ourselves against others, we are using embedded norms and practices to assess where we stand.

According to Bill Dressler, cultural consonance is the degree to which individuals, in their own beliefs and behaviors, approximate the prototypes for belief and behavior encoded in cultural models. Low cultural consonance is associated with greater psychological distress and other health outcomes.

The same is true for our relationships. We evaluate our relationships and how they fit into "normal behaviors and practices" around us to gauge what we have with the other person. This starts at a young age and is a characteristic of our sociability as a species. Think of how many times in your childhood you had friends with parents who allowed them to do an activity that your parent(s) did not permit you to do and vice-versa. The infamous, "But Susie's parents are letting her go, so why can't I?" question is rooted in comparison and is a prime example of how we compare norms and relationship activities to others.

The challenging part is that we share a common macro-culture but have individual sub-cultures that contribute to our personal value system and how we approach everyday life. Regardless of what domain you're in, blending subcultures that you're a part of should include elements that are in common with your value system that require clarity on exactly who you are, what you stand for, and what your purpose is. The tough part is having the clarity to know when a relationship doesn't align with your value system but walking away from it might diminish your reputation in the eyes of others you share a subculture with. Dealing with the judgement of others for not aligning ourselves in a way that they believe we should can cause disparity in our confidence and challenge our understanding of the right course of action.

For example, how many people do you know who are married (or in a long-term relationship) and are miserable? They complain about their partner, constantly highlight their pitfalls instead of praising their wins, yet they stay with them and act like everything is great whenever they're around that person. How is this possible? How can we pretend happiness when we're burning with anguish and frustration? This is due to fear. Fear of what we and others may think of becoming divorced or separated and holding onto a silent hope that things will change and get better.

These are cultural norms at work. The fear of having others judge your separation is a byproduct of your desire to blend in and be accepted, not only because of others but also because of your own self-esteem and belief in the way you see yourself in the relationship. Fear can be a tricky thing to overcome, and as an old mentor of mine once said, "I have no time for fear. It literally serves no functional purpose. What has to get done needs to get done." The same applies to relationships and knowing when it's time to walk away.

You must embrace the fact that things are going to change; people change, you change, circumstances change. It's inevitable; yet, because we become conditioned to viewing and feeling things in a particular way that fits with the life we've envisioned for ourselves, we do a very poor job of accepting change or things not going as we expected. So, how do you fix this? *You must find comfort in discomfort.*

Think of going to the gym with the goal of getting into the best shape of your life. What does it take? A lot of discomfort, discipline, and consistency. It's a never-ending process that requires pain because your body is changing and adapting to the demands you're putting it through. Remaining open to the possibility of change within relationships works the same way, minus the gym membership and strict diet.

One of the most incredible characteristics of being human is our ability to think, "What if …". Exploring and imagining possibilities for ourselves and relationships in our lives is a special ability that no other mammal can do. When thinking about these possibilities, we ignore the cost to our own identity as the exchange that will take place with the other individual will undoubtedly include things that we're unprepared for.

We get caught in cyclical patterns with others that keep us from growth, and the only way to recognize that the pattern exists is to step outside of it and have the confidence and fortitude to challenge it. Anything less leads to second-guessing our decisions, as well as the value we place on our time and how we invest it with others.

As time passes and you choose to stay in relationships that are not conducive to your growth, happiness, and fulfillment, you begin to enter a realm of degrading your self-worth. Many of us don't think of it this way; we focus on how others will perceive us and are bound by the fear of not living up to the expectations we initially established for the relationship. Or, we remain in a relationship for what we can get out of it at the cost of our own happiness and fulfillment, which isn't good, either.

Remember, change affects each of us. You can embrace the change now, or you can deal with the consequences of not allowing yourself positive growth, which will diminish your mental, emotional, and spiritual health. If you stay in that cycle long enough, long-standing personality shifts become a possibility, which lends itself to losing other relationships that truly contribute to your fulfillment and identity, something we don't often consider. Since they're always there, we take those dependable relationships for granted.

Remember, you're not staying in a misaligned relationship because of the other person, you're staying because of the "normal" you've established with that relationship and are fearful of what life looks like without it. Walking away will be scary, but nowhere near as scary as what you'll become if you continue to deprive yourself of growth and limit the possibilities of what your life could be when you fulfill the purpose you were designed for.

You were made to be extraordinary. You were made to savor every second of sweet air you get the opportunity to breathe. You were made to be a positive influence on others, and you can only achieve that by having the discipline to influence yourself to be authentically happy and genuine in everything you do.

What Life Looks Like When You Limit Possibilities

It's heartbreaking when you see people put on different faces across the different relationships they're in. They bend their morals, ethics, personality, etc., to suit the needs of the person directly in front of them as they attempt to maintain continuity with what they perceive the relationship's benefits to be. I had a friend who used to do this with her boyfriend all the time. She would be her authentic and genuine self around family and friends, but whenever he was around, her entire demeanor and how she held herself changed. She changed her word choices, diminished the level of excitement she displayed about things she was passionate about and tolerated a level of disrespect from him that she would never tolerate from others. She literally sacrificed the very essence of who she genuinely was out of fear of making him upset and what he would do to her if they separated.

This is not the way to garner, build, and maintain a healthy relationship, but it's done every day all over the world. So, what's the cost? What is the actual cost of closing off possibilities and becoming entrapped in self-stagnation? In the renowned text, "The Top Five Regrets of Dying," palliative care nurse Bronnie Ware compiled common regrets that individuals shared as they faced their final days on earth. These top five regrets were:

1. *I wish I'd had the courage to live a life true to myself, not the life others expected of me.*
2. *I wish I hadn't worked so hard.*
3. *I wish I'd had the courage to express my feelings.*
4. *I wish I had stayed in touch with my friends.*
5. *I wish that I had let myself be happier.*

What is the common theme of all five? A lack of belief in oneself to accept other possibilities besides a life filled with conditioned norms that limit the importance of positive change through exploration of "what could be."

What would keep someone from living a life of authentic truth and dismissing the expectations of what others believe their life should be? Why would someone dedicate their precious time to working so hard at the expense of their own health and happiness? What would make someone lack the confidence to express their feelings? What life circumstances arise that reduce the importance of good friendships? Why in the world would someone not strive to be as happy as possible in life?

These are the result of self-imposed limitations and finding comfort within a conditioned norm only to recognize that the comfort is also the shackle that keeps you from seeing things a different way, which could lead to a new world of happiness, fulfillment of purpose, and optimal impact in all relationships.

How many people live a life filled with regret and never recognize it until they're on their death bed? *Statistics show that over 90% of people live with immense regret from missed opportunities.* This is a serious problem that doesn't get the attention it should because of one simple reason: it's difficult. *It's difficult to be raw, honest, and deliberate with yourself about self-imposed limitations because it's always easier to blame circumstances and other people rather than our own personal constraints.*

Your brain does not like accepting that it messed up because that means an inefficiency occurred and came with a very real cost to your personal fulfillment that can only be associated with the choices and decisions you did or did not make.

Challenging ourselves to push past what we think is possible is exactly what needs to be done. This means questioning the way you think your life is supposed to be lived, the way you interact with others, and why you interact with them. It also means analyzing your ability to make quality decisions based on fulfillment rather than meeting a culturally-imposed norm that may never have made sense to you, but that you adopted to achieve consonance. This goes against the grain of standardization and dares yourself to be extraordinary so that you can live a life of purpose, difference, and meaning.

This is the nature of creating relationships with real impact: influencing one life at a time through decisions, choices, and understandings that supersede what norms are to show what is truly possible. You, like everyone else, thirst for fulfillment, excitement, love, passion, and meaning. How can living a life filled with the regret of "would've, should've, could've" get you there? It can't. You must force yourself to make the harder choice and go against the grain that tells you that you must do "x, y, and z" to be socially accepted and self-fulfilled. Without it, you'll never reach the potential you have within, which means that the relationships you're committed to will never be everything they possibly can be.

I've never met a person who didn't want to have the absolute best relationship possible with their spouse, children, family members, friends, co-workers, etc. The consistent challenge is in not knowing how to make those relationships their best. The only way to achieve it is by opening yourself to the possibilities of what *your* best is so that you can help bring out the best in others.

LAYER SEVEN:
Self-Regulation

Strive for Balance

Maintaining balance throughout life is a challenge. There are pinnacles and valleys that must constantly be endured, and finding the right method for regulation requires a deeper understanding than we're currently conditioned for. As a dear mentor of mine, Dr. Bob Parrino, once told me, "Life is a rollercoaster; as fast as you make it to the top, you'll be dropping to the bottom and repeating the process over and over again until the ride eventually stops." *Finding comfort in knowing that there will always be unexpected twists and turns is a fundamental component of having balance in your life; always expect the unexpected and never underestimate any life circumstance or relationship.*

Major religions and spiritual studies throughout the world address the concept of self-regulation and balance in different ways. The Buddhist religion calls this Tatramajjhattatā, or equanimity and balance of mind. The Sikh religion calls followers to "Live in the world, yet keep your mind pure" through balance of time and suspension of pride, lust, anger, greed, and worldly attachment. The Christian faith calls believers to live a life rooted in dedication, hard work, consistent faith, and detachment from worldly things to prevent idolization and manipulation of oneself.

Seeking a well-regulated life (and working toward it) has been a goal of our species for thousands of years, particularly since we attained a point in our existence where self-actualization was able to become a priority and focus.

In the relationships we commit and devote ourselves to there has to be a clear understanding of our intentions. You must know why you're there. What is it about the person that pulls you to them? What good do they facilitate in your life, and is it something attached to your core values and identity or is it superficial because you simply want something out of the person, or you like something the person does for you? If it's the latter, there's an immediate need to address your own priorities and self-worth as it signifies that there's work to be done with balancing yourself so that you can balance everything in your life.

You should never look to others to make you feel better about yourself; that should come from within and be a byproduct of the discoveries you've made about who you are and what you stand for.

Self-Regulation Starts with Self-Care

As best-selling author, Dr. Joe Dispenza, stated in a recent interview, "Work on yourself instead of turning your relationship into work. This will allow the relationship to flow." Working on ourselves means that we care enough about our well-being that we're willing to push past our comfort zones to "put in the work." This facilitates growth past limitations and models that are no longer productive for the circumstances of our lives. This is synonymous with the cliché, "Out with the old; in with the new." It takes work to purge old habits, perspectives and emotional stagnation that perhaps served us at one point but are no longer productive.

Most people consider "self-care" to be a day at the spa, taking a vacation, going to the gym regularly, eating healthily, etc., and these are all good, but rarely is self-care aligned with hard work and making tough decisions in how we think about ourselves, what we expect of others, and working toward eliminating our own biases. Pushing the bounds of your own understanding means being willing and able to adapt to the never-ending changes that life will undoubtedly throw your way. What greater gift could you give yourself?

It's important to equip your heart, mind, and soul with the discipline to find solace and accept life's circumstances without turning to someone else to provide that for you. To achieve success in any relationship, we need to recognize when we're not self-aligned, let alone aligned with another person.

You don't latch onto someone else in an attempt to fill gaps in your own self-awareness and understanding. You must care enough about yourself to accept who you truly are and who you are not so you can make appropriate decisions that facilitate self-regulation with more ease as each year goes by. Anything short of this means you're doing it wrong.

When we say that we "love ourselves," we should ask how much "tough self-love" we give. Think of some of the most important life lessons you've endured. Somewhere along the way, tough love played a role to get you back on your feet and through whatever adversity you were facing. It could have come from a parent, sibling, coach, family member, or any other person you were willing to accept influence and direction from. When you make any changes to your lifestyle, it requires an adjustment period. That adjustment period is uncomfortable, and it's supposed to be. You wouldn't be doing something different if it wasn't uncomfortable because it means nothing would actually be changing.

Starting a new diet, a new workout, a new job, living in a new place, all require adjustment periods before they become a normal part of your routine. *Commitment to change is a huge part of tough self-love.* You must be committed in a way that isn't tied to seeing immediate change or real-time feedback, which means you have to be willing to fight for it and go the distance. This requires patience, discipline, temperance, and dedication to instill objective truths within your mind that will lead to different outcomes and greater understanding of yourself and the relationships you're committed to.

Think about Layer Six and how many people stay in committed relationships out of fear. Fear of having "wasted their time" if they walk away, fear of not knowing what life will look like without that person always there, fear of not having the economic benefits of being with that person, and fear of what others may think about them walking away. This is heartbreaking and an absolute travesty. While I am not recommending that you quickly walk away from deeply committed relationships, I am recommending you self-evaluate once you start feeling like the relationship is red-lining.

Recall what made you commit to the relationship in the first place and whether your intentions or the other person's intentions have changed. In a relationship, growth never happens in a straight line. It is a plethora of mazes with surprise doors and booby traps that gradually progress upward. It takes both people involved in the relationship to be committed to figuring out how to get through it. It cannot be a one-sided journey. When it starts to feel as though it is, you need to know why. The only way to know why is to know yourself and what decisions you've made that ultimately started to make you feel this way.

Did you tolerate something you shouldn't have? Did you push a bunch of little things to the side that have now built up and are casting a shadow on your happiness and fulfillment? Did you hold back from expressing feelings to the other person because you didn't want to upset them? These are all minor examples of things that don't reflect self-care as they were moments you didn't display love and respect for yourself. You didn't meet the challenge to do the harder thing and sacrificed your own worth to appease the other person.

You need to care about yourself enough to speak your truth and not allow negative emotions and thoughts to build up inside. Once the buildup starts, you begin to lose the ability to be objective and self-regulate. There's no way you can be objective and have clarity when you're deprived. It's simply impossible and puts the responsibility on someone else to satisfy that deprivation. *The reality is that you can and should fill your own deprivations.*

Regulating Stress

Stress is a fact of life. Whether it is stress regarding other people, your performance with a particular task, or life circumstances in general, you'll always deal with some level of stress and that's not always a bad thing. Stress can be a motivator and an ally if it's perceived correctly and utilized properly. The challenge most of us face is when negative stress becomes a defining element in our everyday lives that consumes us and doesn't allow us to stop, breathe, and objectively assess why we're enduring the stress in the first place.

Feeling stress means that something must change or be responded to. It's a catalyst, pressuring you to do something that perhaps you don't want to do but must be done. For example, the stress I feel when having to fire an employee will be different from the stress I feel when running late to a family dinner. Both are stressors, but they have different applications in my life. The part that matters is the *how*. *How* do you deal with life's variables and the curveballs that conjure stress? *How* do you shift your mentality to perceive stress as a growth opportunity and a tool for you to learn more about yourself? This requires understanding the effects of the stress that you allow into your heart and mind, and the influence that it has on your quality of life. In the world of medical research, this is called allostasis and allostatic load.

According to Merriam-Webster, allostasis is the process by which a state of internal, physiological equilibrium is maintained by an organism in response to actual or perceived environmental and psychological stressors.

According to the International Encyclopedia of the Social & Behavioral Sciences, allostatic load is the cost of chronic exposure to elevated or fluctuating endocrine or neural responses resulting from chronic or repeated challenges that the individual experiences as stressful.

These terms create the framework of how stress effects your balance/equilibrium as well as its long-term effects throughout your body.

Our society lives in an incredible state of chronic stress. We have stimuli everywhere, and only give ourselves a short amount of time to figure something out or make decisions. This is haphazard, as we are not conditioned to think thoroughly under chronic pressure that could end up being detrimental to us in the long run. This conditioning carries over into our personal lives and affects the quality of the decisions we make.

A vast majority of us believe this is tied solely to the information and digital age, but they're wrong. This shift goes back to the industrial revolution and the idea that there are processes and standard templates for doing something that will produce mass results. Applying this "push button" framing to relationships and negotiating the inner wilderness that is yourself is dangerous. Any time there's a "push button" process that relies on standardization, there are details, nuances, and niches that are missed. When understanding how we make decisions for ourselves that impact how we regulate stress and what we find stressful, this matters.

Our thoughts and decisions have become conditioned to operate at such a fast pace that we don't have any expectation of being able to stop, breathe, and listen to discern why we're stressed while identifying the best way to manage varying stress loads.

It's amazing what a simple Google search of "stress relief" will show. Everything from diets to supplements to exercise routines, as well as meditation techniques, among a few others. Unfortunately, you'll rarely find "introspective reflection" or "self-assessment" to uncover why you're allowing the stressor to have a profound effect on you. In the quest for self-regulation, this is crucial. *You can do things all day that alter your response to a stressor without addressing the root causes of how or why you're mismanaging the stress around you.*

I can live my entire life addressing symptoms without ever removing the disease that causes the symptoms, and you don't want to live life merely responding to symptoms. *You want to recognize the cause of the perceived stress so you can either reframe it or eliminate it.* This is not to say that you won't have moments that knock you out of equilibrium due to an unexpected stressor that effects your well-being; this happens to all of us. What I want you to do is have a clear understanding of how that stressor is going to make you a better, stronger, and a more solid human being so you can be a light within the relationships you have now and in the future.

I spent seven years of my career researching how stress in combat affects military members. I took a deep dive into the details of life-or-death situations and how they impacted service members in their domestic relationships. Through participant observation, focus groups, and interviews, I followed progress and growth for some, as well as relationship digression and separation for others. Most folks across the world have minimal to no experience with facing life-or-death situations on a regular basis. It's the real reason why our species adapted a stress response system, so it could respond to a stressor in an effort to keep us alive (Sapolsky 1994).

The release of the neurohormones epinephrine, norepinephrine, and cortisol serve important functions in giving our bodies the ability to do extreme things in dire circumstances. These responses expend a ton of energy and are not longitudinally sustainable but have a strong impact in the function and capacity of our internal organs, neurocircuitry, and psychological health.

For military members who used loss, adversity, dislocation, and lived violence as a tool to appreciate the relationships they had at home, they often experienced growth and continued progression with their loved ones. For those who dwelled on the combative stress experience and consistently held onto the violence they participated in, the lives that were lost, and the mistakes that were made, there was a profound disconnect that took place with their ability to reconnect with their relationships at home. This is understandable as grave trauma can have an isolating effect where individuals separate themselves from others and use language like, "You just wouldn't understand," "You had to be there," and the like due to their moral and psychological injury.

This creates a gap between what is actually stressful and what is being perceived as stressful. This distinction is important. For those of us who have never or will never experience such circumstances, it's easy to get caught up in perceived stressors that shouldn't warrant a full-blown stress response, yet we have them anyway. Recognizing and controlling this is part of self-regulation. You need to know what actually matters in your purpose and existence as living in a state of constant stress or overreaction will build barriers between you and others.

Regardless of whether it's combat or being stuck in traffic and running late for work, the same biological stress response is taking place. Your hypothalamus, pituitary, and adrenal glands become activated and secrete neurohormones that increase your heart rate and respiration, creating a feeling of heaviness in your chest. This is your body going into "fight, flight, or freeze" mode, which is something our bodies have as a survival response specifically for life-or-death situations. The key words here are "life-or-death."

For combat military members, first responders, civilians caught in a war zone, etc., this response makes sense. *For the rest of us who don't face these sorts of circumstances, this response is a misuse of our biology triggered and controlled by perceived danger and stress within our brains.* There are countless examples of this throughout today's society. Stress that is felt when a police officer gets behind you and puts his lights on, yet you know you've done nothing wrong and perhaps he's getting ready to pass you; stress you feel when you don't get a certain number of likes and comments on a social media post when it has nothing to do with your physical safety; stress we feel when waiting in a long line at the grocery store, etc. The examples are limitless.

Most of us in the industrialized West live a life of privilege and want for nothing as far as the necessities for basic survival are concerned. This has shifted our use of the stress response system to things that we perceive as vital and crucial within our value system that relate to social standing among our peers as well as our relationships.

A recent poll conducted by Pew Research showed that over 70% of Americans utilize social media and experience more stress because of it. The stress contributed to the "cost of caring" phenomenon in which users of social media became distressed when seeing constant hardship or negativity posted by other users on the network. This makes sense.

We are communal and tribal by nature, so something that affects one of us has the potential to affect all of us (if we let it). The person experiencing stress is not the one living in the situation, they're reading about it or watching a video of someone else who is. What they do with that information as soon as it crosses their filters of perception will either trigger emotional compromise and engage meaning or they will pay no mind to it and go about their day.

What has been found is that most individuals carry the stress of others throughout their day, which has a very real effect and influence on the way they see the world and their ability to regulate their emotions and thoughts. These doses of perceived stress over things that don't directly play into their well-being can cause a lot of challenges if they are consistently consumed, which is happening more often as most people spend well over three hours a day on social media. These platforms are influencing our emotions, inner thoughts and ability to regulate expectations in relationships which have biological consequences with neurohormone regulation, mental health, and stress management.

Influence Yourself So You Can Influence Others

The ancient Japanese believed in three major tenants of leadership that I follow and contribute to applied mindfulness and self-regulation:

1. Mushin: Achieving a state of "no mind"
2. Zanshin: Achieving a state of being fully aware of your surroundings
3. Fudoshin: Achieving a state of complete emotional balance

The concept of *Mushin* (as mentioned in Layer Four) means to have complete stillness in your mind. Not looking ahead, not looking in the past, simply being in the present with no distractions. When we talk about concepts such as equilibrium, values, and purpose, achieving a state of "no mind" is where you want to be so you can turn down the noise of everything in your life and provide a stillness that will encourage your inner truth to make itself known.

Society encourages us to move ten steps ahead without recognizing that the second step is influenced by the outcome of the first step, and so on. Striving to silence distracting thoughts and society's expectations, even temporarily, will serve you well as it makes you question yourself instead of going through the motions and doing what norms have conditioned you to do. *It is one thing do something; it's another thing to understand why you're doing it.*

The concept of *Zanshin* goes hand in hand with *Mushin*. Having stillness of mind allows you to reach a level of vigilance and awareness that is simply not achievable when you're occupied with what your environment and surroundings looked like in the past and predicting what they'll look like in the future. When managing and leading yourself through life, as well as relationships, we must be aware of every detail, every move, and every emotion so you can make sound, informed decisions. *Being able to make successful, productive decisions in a relationship demands that you make productive decisions for yourself; the framing is exactly the same.*

To optimize the effects of *Mushin* and *Zanshin*, *Fudoshin* is a necessity. Your emotions are an incredibly powerful tool that can work for you or against you and the influence you strive to have for positive outcomes within your life. Achieving *Fudoshin* means that you're not easily shaken. When it comes to your emotional equilibrium, you're an oak tree rather than a willow tree. Regardless of circumstances, consequences, or outcomes, you maintain emotional balance. This absoluteness signifies confidence. *If you have confidence, you have belief; and if you have belief, you know that you're worthy of believing in.*

When you combine these pillars together, you start acquiring ingredients that contribute to your understanding of leadership and what it means to influence yourself before influencing others. *You could read a million books about leadership and try every new strategy or technique, but until you fully embrace what it means to have a top-down relationship with yourself, you will never be able to guide and lead the human condition in a manner that is effective, productive, and sustainable.*

Organize Your Relationships

Have you visualized all the relationships in your life? Most of us have never done this and we miss out on so much because of it. You visualize your financial investments, goals, calendar, plans for the future, and so many other things that mean a lot to you. Yet, the relationships we invest irreplaceable time in never seem to make the cut of things that are a priority and worthy of intentional thought and meaning. This exercise is called *mind mapping*, and its purpose is to recognize not just *who* but *why* you've committed to relationships and how those relationships influence your life. It's used throughout the discipline of human behavior and creates a visual representation of an intangible. Your relationships are to be valued, just as the time you spend investing in them is to be valued. On the following page is a brief template you can use to begin creating your own mind map to highlight the bank of relationships that make up your social capital:

Seven Layers of Successful Relationships

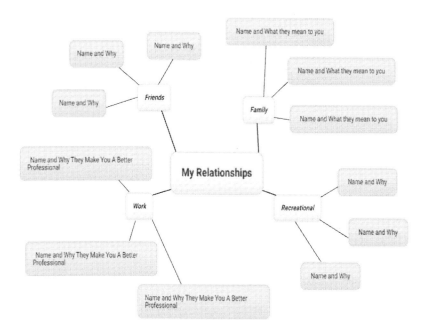

Give it a try. You'll need to customize your relationship map to include your specific life domains. Add in every social sphere you're involved in and the relationships that define the people within that domain. Visualize your relationships so that you can cross-reference them with your personal value system. Do each of them fall in line with your values and reinforce them? Do some of them challenge your values? Do they make life a little bit easier or a bit harder? Do they reinforce your personal constitution in a way that feeds your life's purpose? These are all questions that must be explored and understood.

This visualization provides a tool for you to use as an evaluation metric, as well. Next to each person, put a number you associate with them that runs off a Likert scale. Use the number *1* for relationships that have no positive value within that particular domain of your life and a *10* for relationships that make up a large part of what you identify with in that domain. All the numbers in between will serve as degrees of how much you value the relationship.

Once you understand the dynamics and value of each relationship, it's time to start making some decisions about what to do with them.

Self-regulation requires clarity and transparency; clarity within your life and transparency with others who make up the bank of relationships in your life. We understand that we are social creatures tied by tribal associations that are rooted in bonds. These bonds rely on trust and authenticity.

Your ability to regulate your emotions, commitments, and differing perspectives will depict the level of trust you're willing to give as well as the depth of authenticity you bring to each relationship you commit to. Without these, stress will inadvertently increase as you find yourself getting involved in relationships that don't speak to your heart; rather, they speak to the ebb and flow of figuring out how to regulate yourself, which does not equate to creating successful relationships that are aligned with who you are and were meant to be.

That is what self-regulation is: tempering what you need vs. what you want (and understanding the difference between the two), who you choose to be around and why, as well as recognizing when it's time to make shifts and changes to maintain equilibrium (or achieve it). You need to know what feeds your vulnerabilities that make regulating your thoughts, feelings, and actions challenging. *Many times, it's those around us who keep us vulnerable instead of fortifying our confidence and belief in what we were made to be.* The negativity, toxicity, and control others can have in our lives requires us to regulate how much time we spend with them as well as what we're willing to give them.

Remember, the most valuable thing that exists on this earth is your time. Once you deposit it, you can never get it back, and who you deposit it with can shape or break the understanding you have of yourself and what your true purpose is. Use this tool to evaluate who is worth your time and develop a clear understanding of how they make you better and how you make them better. If you can't easily find that answer, then it's time to question why you're involved in that relationship.

Full Circle: Meshing Layers

There's a lot more to making relationships successful outside of having more conversations with people you seek relationships with. Success within a relationship starts with success in understanding yourself, your purpose, and what you need to reach fulfillment as a human being. You're going to have to ask yourself hard questions and work through hurdles to find the answers.

There's an entire industry devoted to fortifying relationships through team-building exercises, counseling services, personality assessments, and other methodologies. These are great tools to have at your disposal, but *a sustainable first step toward success with others begins with recognizing the disparities, gaps, and deprivations that live within yourself.* This recognition will tell you a lot about your beliefs, your values, and how you've made sense of the experiences you've lived and the impact previous learning has had on your present understanding of life.

Until you begin this journey, you'll have challenges in relationships. They may be silent challenges that you don't share with others, but the thorns they produce will exist and create space that will not allow the cohesion and continuity you deserve.

Life is simply too short to rely solely on others for validation. You need to learn how to rely on yourself so you can contribute to relationships and generate a mutual flow with the person you choose to relate with. We often don't do this. *We enter into relationships to fill voids or satisfy particular needs that are a product of our own deprivations.* This means that you'll align yourself with someone to fill that void rather than aligning yourself with someone so that you can complement each other. The difference between the two is that one is sustainable while the other is not.

There is a shelf-life involved when relationships are misaligned, which often ends in full blowouts with messy strings attached. We want to avoid these as they can be traumatic. They distort our perceptions of the other person, which makes us question our judgment and ask things like, "Why didn't I see this coming?" The reality is that subconsciously, you did, but you chose not to recognize it because the void the other person filled provided temporary satisfaction. But it did not cure the root of the deprivation; only you can do that.

This book has been written to get you closer to yourself. It's the only way you'll be able to open up and get closer to others and create the life you deserve with the people that belong in it. We all spend an immense amount of time sifting through distractions and stimuli that put distance between who we once were, who we are, and who we strive to be. *Who you choose to have in your corner when sifting through the many chapters of life will build you into the person you want to be or break you down into the failure you fear to be.* This is important, so give yourself the time you deserve.

Study the diagram on the next page. The beginnings of any relationship start with you and your relationship with yourself. Your personal understanding of your value, worth, and purpose is a direct reflection of what you believe as far as where you come from, which represents the Source that made you. This Source will drive your purpose, which fosters your ability to guide who you should align with. Once aligned, give yourself and the other person an opportunity to listen (not to be confused with *hear*). As you listen, connect dots to establish a next step, since every relationship should be growth-centric and allow you to stay open to possibilities for you and the other person. Being able to self-regulate your emotions and reactions will allow you to sustain the relationship while maintaining equilibrium within your own constitution so you can consistently strive for growth and greater understanding of yourself and those you seek to relate with.

Seven Layers of Successful Relationships

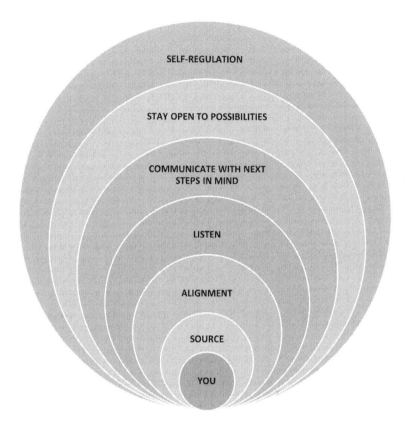

This is how it's done, but it starts with YOU.

Care enough to invest in yourself. Care enough to value your irreplaceable worth. Commit yourself to growth and understanding so that you can better understand others and achieve success in the exchange and interplay that is human relations.

The Next Step

Those of us who are fortunate enough to not die unexpectedly, whether through an accident, natural catastrophe, etc., live an average of 73 to 80 years. Most people don't like to think about this but you started to die the moment you came into this world and were given life. Each moment that passed, every day that went by, every week, every month, every year that you've lived cannot be re-lived. Every word that comes out of your mouth cannot not be deleted and rephrased. Every action you've committed is etched into the history of who you are. We don't have the ability to go back and take advantage of missed opportunities.

As it relates to time, there are no opportunities for a re-do; there are no second takes, or do overs. There is a date and time when you will cease to be on this earth and our days are numbered.

How much longer will you waste precious time doing things that don't pertain to your truth?

> "Men talk of killing time, while
> time quietly kills them."
>
> DION BOUCICAULT

I urge you to stop devaluing your very existence by living your life on autopilot. You deserve much more out of life but it's up to you to go get it. Through this book, you know how to successfully understand who you are and what you represent.

I've given you tools to open up a freeway of communication with others as well as yourself. Take control of your actions and start being comfortable with the ambiguity of tomorrow. Contrary to popular belief, time is not on your side. We are amazing and yet fragile beings with a shelf life.

Your relationships define you. *People are the witnesses of your existence.* If a man was born on Mars and we never knew him or knew others who could witness his life and death, what would he matter to you? He wouldn't. How did he affect you? He didn't. He couldn't. But you, you have people all around you. You have the power to influence them and make them feel something.

Ask yourself this question: How do you want to make the next person you talk to feel? Whatever the answer is, I want you to know, as certain as you are breathing, that you have the power to do it.

As a species we learn by imitating others. I may do some things my great, great, great grandfather did, although I never met him. However, the actions he did and his mannerisms were mimicked by his son, and his son after him, and his son after him, and my dad. You were born with a collective conscious that has been handed down through the halls of time.

While that's awesome to feel connected to your forefathers, not every trait that was passed down is a good trait. Every person carries shackles of dead weight. Some, we brought upon by ourselves, while others we mimicked, and others were handed down from generation to generation. The good news is, you can create new habits and teach your children as well as others a better way to go through life, and there is nothing more fulfilling than that.

Harness the power of connectivity with other people by establishing rich, and meaningful relationships. You can do that by being confident in who you are and who you are not. People who have toxic relationships with themselves as well as others cringe inwardly when they realize their to-do list for the day. Conversely, people who know themselves and their worth take in a deep breath of life in the mornings and make every person they run into, feel them.

I have peeled back the layers of misconceptions you may have had of yourself and others. You are now equipped to lower the volume on all of life's noises so that you can hear your true self speak. Once you hear you, give others the gift of hearing you too! Genuine, truthful, and authentic connection defines the beautiful sweetness of life. Without it, life is sour, bitter.

Close your eyes and imagine yourself twelve months from today, the day you told yourself that you are going to live your truth out loud with yourself and others. Go ahead, close your eyes and envision yourself and the relationships that mean the most to you, the book will be here when you reopen them.

Are you genuinely happy and fulfilled?
What relationships are there? What do they look like?
How are your conversations different?
Which relationships are gone? Why did they need to leave?
What new relationships exist?
Who calls you? Who do you text?
Where do you spend your free time and whom do you spend your free time with? Have you reconnected with long-lost friends and family members?
Do you smile more, laugh more, and stress less?

You can have all of that and more, now that you know what to do and how to do it right.

Like all things, this book must also come to an end. Believe me when I tell you, whether I know you or not, I am honored and humbled that you've read this book. I pray that it has deposited seeds in you that will result in good, healthy fruit.

If you'd like to go deeper with me, I invite you to visit this book's website – www.se7enlayers.com or visit my Facebook page, @ drginocollura, where I do live teachings periodically, mentor, and answer questions.

I invite you to continue this journey that you have started with me. I'm available to speak to any group that is in need of motivation, clarity, encouragement, and understanding so they can recapture the luster for their lives and connections with others.

My friend, I pray that success and happiness meet you every day of your life and that you can shine the beautiful light that is you into others so you leave a legacy that will never be mistaken or forgotten.

About The Author

Gino Collura is a behavioral scientist and serial entrepreneur. He is known for being a "go-to" for "C" suite professionals when it comes to navigating the waters of engagement/commitment, influential leadership, as well as internal/external relationship management.

Gino is an accomplished motivational speaker and has had the privilege of speaking to business owners, empowerment groups, professional associations, and students across the globe.

He was born and raised in Tampa, Florida and has been there the majority of his life minus a three-year stint where he lived and worked in South America as an Anti-Kidnapping specialist. That period was an experience that changed his life forever and opened the gateway to his passion for understanding others, why they do the things they do, and influencing them to make positive as well as sustainable changes in their lives.

As a peer-reviewed author as well as PhD in the field of Neuroanthropology, he has dedicated his life's work to enhancing the quality and impact groups and individuals have with the minimal time they have on this earth.

Dr. Collura currently resides in Tampa with his beautiful wife, his angel of a daughter and their two dogs, Boone (Chocolate Labrador) and Kaper (Chihuahua).

Acknowledgments

It is with an appreciative heart and sound mind that I acknowledge the following individuals who have helped me grow as a behavioral scientist: Dr. Bob Parrino, Dr. Daniel Lende, Dr. David Himmelgreen, Dr. Matthew Diomede, Dr. Dick Puglisi, and Dr. Bill Anton. Without their belief and investment in me, I would not have the impact on the individuals I've been called to serve. I humbly thank you all.

To every single person and organization who has entrusted me with your betterment, well-being, and growth I cannot thank you enough for your faith, trust and commitment in walking the journey with me. I assure you that I have learned more from you than you have from me.

To my mother, father, wife and daughter, you all are my air and I am blessed and humbled to have been given you.

References

Anton, B. (2015) Ascend: Forging a Path to Your Truer Self. Tampa: HD Interactive.

Chartrand, T. and Bargh J. (1999) The chameleon effect: the perception-behavior link and social interaction. Journal of Personality and Social Psychology, 76(6): 893-910.

Collura, G. and Lende, D. (2012) Post-traumatic Stress Disorder and Neuroanthropology: Stopping PTSD Before it Begins. Annals of Anthropological Practice, 36(1), 131–148.

Dent, N. and O'Hagan, T. (1998) Rousseau on Amour-Propre. Proceedings of the Aristotelian Society, 72: 57–75.

Engel, S., Berkowitz, G., Wolff, M. and Yehuda, R. (2005) Psychological Trauma Associated with the World Trade Center Attacks and its Effect on Pregnancy Outcome. Pediatric and Perinatal Epidemiology, 19: 334-341.

Goodman, A. and Leatherman, T. (1998) Building a New Biocultural Synthesis: Political-Economic Perspectives on Human

Biology (Linking Levels of Analysis). Ann Arbor: University of Michigan Press.

Helfrich, H. (1999) Beyond the Dilemma of Cross-Cultural Psychology: Resolving the Tension Between Etic and Emic Approaches. Culture & Psychology, 5(2): 131–153.

Kirmayer, L. (2007) Psychotherapy and the Cultural Concept of the Person. Transcultural Psychiatry 44 (2): 232-257.

Kondo, D. (1990) Crafting selves: Power, Gender, and Discourses of Identity in a Japanese Workplace. Chicago: University of Chicago Press.

Lewis, R. (2018) Finding Purpose in a Godless World: Why We Care Even If The Universe Doesn't. Amherst, NY: Prometheus Books.

Lindholm, C. (2007) Culture and Identity: The History, Theory, and Practice of Psychological Anthropology. Oxford: Oneworld Publications Limited.

Mackinnon, K., and Fuentes, A. (2012) Primate Social Cognition, Human Evolution, and Niche Construction: A Core Context for Neuroanthropology. In the Encultured Brain eds. Pp. 67-102. Cambridge: MIT Press.

McEwen, B.S. and Seeman, T. (1999) Protective and Damaging Effects of Mediators of Stress: Elaborating and Testing the Concepts of Allostasis and Allostatic Load. Annals of the New York Academy of Sciences, 896: 30-47.

Murphy, F., Nimmo-Smith, I., and Lawrence, A. (2003) Functional Neuroanatomy of Emotions: A Meta-Analysis. Cognitive, Affective, & Behavioral Neuroscience 3 (3): 207-233.

Némedi, D. (1995) Collective Consciousness, Morphology, and Collective Representations: Durkheim's Sociology of Knowledge, 1894–1900. Sociological Perspectives, 38(1):41-56.

Neugarten, B. L. (1979) Time, Age, and the Life Cycle. The American Journal of Psychiatry, 136(7): 887–894.

Obeyesekere, G. (1981) Medusa's Hair: An Essay on Personal Symbols and Religious Experience. Chicago: University of Chicago Press.

Ochsner, Kevin., Chopra, S. and Gross, J. (2004) For Better or for Worse: Neural Systems Supporting the Cognitive Down-and Up Regulation of Negative Emotion. Neuroimage 23 (2): 483-499.

Parish, S. (2008) Subjectivity and Suffering in American Culture: Possible Selves. New York: Palgrave Macmillan.

Sapolsky, R. (1998) Why Zebras Don't Get Ulcers: A Guide to Stress, Stress-Related Diseases, and Coping. New York: W.H. Freeman.

Senge, P. (1990) The Fifth Discipline: The Art and Practice of the Learning Organization. Doubleday Publishers.

Tierney, R. (2018) Toward A Model Of Global Meaning Making. Journal of Literacy Research 50 (4):397-422.

Zacharias, R. (2004) The Real Face of Atheism. Grand Rapids, Michigan: BakerBooks.

Recommended Reading

The Encultured Brain: An Introduction
To Neuroanthropology
By **Daniel Lende and Greg Downey**

Ascend: Forging A Path To Your Truer Self
By **William D. Anton, PhD**

Noise
By **Daniel Kahnerman, Oliver Sibony, and Cass Sunstein**

You're Invited
By **Jon Levy**

The Book Of Five Rings
By **Miyamoto Musashi**

Why Zebras Don't Get Ulcers
By **Robert Sapolsky**

Made in the USA
Columbia, SC
07 August 2021